Italian

The Italian Language Learning Guide for Beginners

© Copyright 2020

All Rights Reserved. No part of this book may be reproduced in any form without permission in writing from the author. Reviewers may quote brief passages in reviews.

Disclaimer: No part of this publication may be reproduced or transmitted in any form or by any means, mechanical or electronic, including photocopying or recording, or by any information storage and retrieval system, or transmitted by email without permission in writing from the publisher.

While all attempts have been made to verify the information provided in this publication, neither the author nor the publisher assumes any responsibility for errors, omissions or contrary interpretations of the subject matter herein.

This book is for entertainment purposes only. The views expressed are those of the author alone, and should not be taken as expert instruction or commands. The reader is responsible for his or her own actions.

Adherence to all applicable laws and regulations, including international, federal, state and local laws governing professional licensing, business practices, advertising and all other aspects of doing business in the US, Canada, UK or any other jurisdiction is the sole responsibility of the purchaser or reader.

Neither the author nor the publisher assumes any responsibility or liability whatsoever on the behalf of the purchaser or reader of these materials. Any perceived slight of any individual or organization is purely unintentional.

Contents

PART 1: ITALIAN FOR BEGINNERS 1
INTRODUCTION 2
SECTION 1 – BASIS OF GRAMMAR 5
SECTION 2 – VERBAL SYSTEM 33
SECTION 3 – GRAMMAR EXERCISES 59
SECTION 4 – DIALOGUES 76
SECTION 5 – VOCABULARY 116
5.1 NOUNS AND ADJECTIVES – NOMI E AGGETTIVI 116
5.1.1 NATIONS AND NATIONALITIES – NAZIONI E NAZIONALITÀ .. 116
5.2 MOST COMMONS VERBS – VERBI PIÙ COMUNI 133
ACCENDERE (TO SWITCH ON) 133
[PAST PARTICIPLE "ACCESO"] 133
ACCETTARE (TO ACCEPT) 133
AGGIUSTARE (TO FIX) 133
AIUTARE (TO HELP) 133
ALZARSI (TO WAKE UP) 133
AMARE (TO LOVE) 133
APRIRE (TO OPEN) 133

[PAST PARTICIPLE "APERTO"] 133
ANDARE (TO GO) 133
[PRESENTE INDICATIVE "IO VADO, TU VAI, EGLI/ELLA VA, NOI ANDIAMO, VOI ANDATE, LORO VANNO] 133
ARRIVARE (TO ARRIVE) 133
ASCOLTARE (TO LISTEN) 133
ASPETTARE (TO WAIT) 134
ATTRAVERSARE (TO CROSS) 134
AVER BISOGNO DI (TO NEED) 134
AVERE CALDO (TO BE HOT) 134
AVERE FAME (TO BE HUNGRY) 134
AVERE FREDDO (TO BE COLD) 134
AVERE PAURA (TO BE SCARED) 134
AVERE RAGIONE (TO BE RIGHT) 134
AVERE SETE (TO BE THIRSTY) 134
AVERE SONNO (TO BE TIRED) 134
AVERE TORTO (TO BE WRONG) 134
BALLARE (TO DANCE) 134
BERE (TO DRINK) 134
[PRESENTE INDICATIVE "IO BEVO, TU BEVI, EGLI/ELLA BEVE, NOI BEVIAMO, VOI BEVETE, LORO BEVONO] 134
BOLLIRE (TO BOIL) 134
CADERE (TO FALL) 134
CAMBIARE (TO CHANGE) 134
CAMMINARE (TO WALK) 134
CANCELLARE (TO CANCEL) 134
CANTARE (TO SING) 134
CAPIRE (TO UNDERSTAND) 134
[PRESENTE INDICATIVE "IO CAPISCO, TU CAPISCI, EGLI/ELLA CAPISCE, NOI CAPIAMO, VOI CAPITE, LORO CAPISCONO] 134
CENARE (TO HAVE DINNER) 134
CHIAMARE (TO CALL) 134

CHIEDERE (TO ASK) 134
[PAST PARTICIPLE "CHIESTO"] 134
CHIUDERE (TO CLOSE) 135
[PAST PARTICIPLE "CHIUSO"] 135
COMINCIARE (TO BEGIN) 135
COMPRARE (TO BUY) 135
CONTARE (TO COUNT) 135
CORRERE (TO RUN) 135
[PAST PARTICIPLE "CORSO"] 135
COSTARE (TO COST) 135
COSTRUIRE (TO BUILD) 135
[PRESENTE INDICATIVE "IO COSTRUISCO, TU COSTRUISCI,
EGLI/ELLA COSTRUISCE, NOI COSTRUIAMO, VOI COSTRUITE,
LORO COSTRUISCONO] 135
CREDERE (TO BELIEVE) 135
CRESCERE (TO GROW) 135
[PRESENTE INDICATIVE "IO CRESCO, TU CRESCI, EGLI/ELLA
CRESCE, NOI CRESCIAMO, VOI CRESCETE, LORO CRESCONO] 135
[PAST PARTICIPLE "CRESCIUTO"] 135
CUOCERE (TO COOK) 135
[PRESENTE INDICATIVE "IO CUOCIO, TU CUOCI, EGLI/ELLA
CUOCE, NOI CUOCIAMO, VOI CUOCETE, LORO CUOCIONO] 135
[PAST PARTICIPLE "COTTO"] 135
DARE (TO GIVE) 135
[PRESENTE INDICATIVE "IO DO, TU DAI, EGLI/ELLA DÀ, NOI
DIAMO, VOI DATE, LORO DANNO] 135
DARE UNA FESTA (TO HAVE A PARTY) 135
DECIDERE (TO DECIDE) 135
[PAST PARTICIPLE "DECISO"] 135
DIMENTICARE (TO FORGET) 135
DIRE (TO SAY/TO TELL) 135
[PRESENTE INDICATIVE "IO DICO, TU DICI, EGLI/ELLA DICE, NOI
DICIAMO, VOI DITE, LORO DICONO] 136

[PAST PARTICIPLE "DETTO"] 136
DIVENTARE (TO BECOME) 136
DIVERTIRSI (TO HAVE FUN) 136
DORMIRE (TO SLEEP) 136
ENTRARE (TO GET IN) 136
FARE (TO DO/TO MAKE) 136
[PRESENTE INDICATIVE "IO FACCIO, TU FAI, EGLI/ELLA FA, NOI FACCIAMO, VOI FATE, LORO FANNO] 136
[PAST PARTICIPLE "FATTO"] 136
FARE COLAZIONE (TO HAVE BREAKFAST) 136
FARSI LA BARBA (TO SHAVE) 136
FARSI LA DOCCIA/IL BAGNO (TO HAVE A SHOWER/A BATH) 136
FARE UN RIPOSINO (TO HAVE A NAP) 136
FERMARSI (TO STOP) 136
FINIRE (TO FINISH/TO END) 136
[PRESENTE INDICATIVE "IO FINISCO, TU FINISCI, EGLI/ELLA FINISCE, NOI FINIAMO, VOI FINITE, LORO FINISCONO] 136
FUMARE (TO SMOKE) 136
GIOCARE (TO PLAY) 136
GIRARE (TO TURN) 136
GUARDARE (TO LOOK) 136
GUIDARE (TO DRIVE) 136
IMPARARE (TO LEARN) 136
INCONTRARE/CONOSCERE (TO MEET) 136
[PRESENTE INDICATIVE "IO CONOSCO, TU CONISCI, EGLI/ELLA CONOSCE, NOI CONOSCIAMO, VOI CONOSCETE, LORO CONSCONO] 136
[PAST PARTICIPLE "CONOSCIUTO"] 137
INDOSSARE (TO WEAR) 137
INSEGNARE (TO TEACH) 137
ISCRIVERSI (TO SIGN UP/TO REGISTER/TO ENROLL) 137
LASCIARE (TO LET/TO LEAVE) 137

LAVARE (TO WASH) 137
LAVORARE (TO WORK) 137
LEGGERE (TO READ) 137
[PAST PARTICIPLE "LETTO"] 137
MANGIARE (TO EAT) 137
MANDARE (TO SEND) 137
MESCOLARE (TO STIR) 137
MORIRE (TO DIE) 137
[PRESENTE INDICATIVE "IO MUOIO, TU MUORI, EGLI/ELLA
MUORE, NOI MORIAMO, VOI MORITE, LORO MUOIONO] 137
[PAST PARTICIPLE "MORTO"] 137
NASCERE (TO BE BORN) 137
[PRESENTE INDICATIVE "IO NASCO, TU NASCI, EGLI/ELLA NASCE,
NOI NASCIAMO, VOI NASCETE, LORO NASCONO] 137
[PAST PARTICIPLE "NATO"] 137
NUOTARE (TO SWIM) 137
OFFRIRE (TO OFFER) 137
[PRESENTE INDICATIVE "IO OFFRO, TU OFFRI, EGLI/ELLA OFFRE,
NOI OFFRIAMO, VOI OFFRITE, LORO OFFRONO] 137
[PAST PARTICIPLE "OFFERTO"] 137
ORDINARE (TO ORDER) 137
PAGARE (TO PAY) 137
PARLARE (TO SPEAK) 137
PARTIRE (TO LEAVE) 138
PASSARE (TO PASS BY) 138
PENSARE (TO THINK) 138
PERDERE/MANCARE (TO LOSE/TO MISS) 138
[PAST PARTICIPLE "PERSO"] 138
PETTINARE (TO COMB) 138
PORTARE (TO BRING) 138
PRANZARE (TO HAVE LUNCH) 138
PRENDERE (TO TAKE) 138

[PAST PARTICIPLE "PRESO"] 138
PREOCCUPARSI (TO WORRY) 138
PREPARARE (TO PREPARE) 138
PULIRE (TO CLEAN) 138
[PRESENTE INDICATIVE "IO PULISCO, TU PULISCI, EGLI/ELLA PULISCE, NOI PULIAMO, VOI PULITE, LORO PULISCONO] 138
RESTARE (TO STAY) 138
[PAST PARTICIPLE "RIMASTO"] 138
RICEVERE (TO RECEIVE) 138
RICORDARE (TO REMEMBER) 138
RIDERE (TO LAUGH) 138
[PAST PARTICIPLE "RISO"] 138
RIEMPIRE (TO FILL) 138
RISPONDERE (TO ANSWER/TO REPLY) 138
[PAST PARTICIPLE "RISPOSTO"] 138
RITORNARE (TO COME BACK) 138
ROMPERE (TO BRAKE) 138
[PAST PARTICIPLE "ROTTO"] 138
RUBARE (TO STEAL) 139
SALIRE (TO COME UP) 139
[PRESENTE INDICATIVE "IO SALGO, TU SALI, EGLI/ELLA SALE, NOI SALIAMO, VOI SALITE, LORO SALGONO] 139
SCEGLIERE (TO CHOOSE) 139
[PRESENTE INDICATIVE "IO SCELGO, TU SCEGLI, EGLI/ELLA SCEGLIE, NOI SCEGLIAMO, VOI SCEGLIETE, LORO SCELGONO] 139
[PAST PARTICIPLE "SCELTO"] 139
SCENDERE (TO CLIMB DOWN/TO GET OFF) 139
[PAST PARTICIPLE "SCESO"] 139
SCRIVERE (TO WRITE) 139
[PAST PARTICIPLE "SCRITTO"] 139
SEMBRARE (TO LOOK LIKE/ TO SEEM LIKE) 139
SENTIRE/PROVARE (TO FEEL) 139

SENTIRE (TO HEAR) 139

SIGNIFICARE (TO MEAN) 139

SOLLEVARE (TO LIFT) 139

SPARIRE (TO DISAPPEAR) 139

[PRESENTE INDICATIVE "IO SPARISCO, TU SPARISCI, EGLI/ELLA SPARISCE, NOI SPARIAMO, VOI SPARITE, LORO SPARISCONO] 139

SPEGNERE (TO SWITCH OFF) 139

[PRESENTE INDICATIVE "IO SPENGO, TU SPEGNI, EGLI/ELLA SPEGNE, NOI SPEGNIAMO, VOI SPEGNETE, LORO SPENGONO] 139

[PAST PARTICIPLE "SPENTO"] 139

SPENDERE/TRASCORRERE (TO SPEND) 139

[PAST PARTICIPLE "SPESO/TRASCORSO"] 139

SPIEGARE (TO EXAPLAIN) 139

SPOSTARE (TO MOVE) 139

STUDIARE (TO STUDY) 140

SUONARE (TO RING/TO PLAY) 140

TAGLIARE (TO CUT) 140

TELEFONARE (TO PHONE) 140

TENERE (TO HOLD/TO KEEP) 140

[PRESENTE INDICATIVE "IO TENGO, TU TIENI, EGLI/ELLA TIENE, NOI TENIAMO, VOI TENETE, LORO TENGONO] 140

TRADURRE (TO TRANSLATE) 140

[PAST PARTICIPLE "TRADOTTO"] 140

TRASLOCARE (TO MOVE – "TO CHANGE PLACE") 140

TROVARE (TO FIND) 140

TRUCCARSI (TO PUT ON MAKEUP) 140

USARE (TO USE) 140

USCIRE (TO GO OUT) 140

[PRESENTE INDICATIVE "IO ESCO, TU ESCI, EGLI/ELLA ESCE, NOI USCIAMO, VOI USCITE, LORO ESCONO] 140

VEDERE (TO SEE/TO WATCH) 140

[PAST PARTICIPLE "VISTO"] 140

VENDERE (TO SELL) 140

VENIRE (TO COME) 140

[PRESENTE INDICATIVE "IO VENGO, TU VIENI, EGLI/ELLA VIENE, NOI VENIAMO, VOI VENITE, LORO VENGONO] 140

VESTIRSI (TO GET DRESSED) 140

VIAGGIARE (TO TRAVEL) 140

VINCERE (TO WIN) 140

[PAST PARTICIPLE "VINTO"] 140

VIVERE (TO LIVE) 140

[PAST PARTICIPLE "VISSUTO"] 140

VOLARE (TO FLY) 141

CONCLUSION 142

PART 2: MASTERING ITALIAN WORDS 144

INTRODUCTION 145

1. AVERE - TO HAVE 150

2. FARE - TO DO/TO MAKE 150

3. ABBASTANZA - ENOUGH 151

4. TROPPO - TOO MUCH 151

5. CIOÈ - IT IS TO SAY 151

6. CHE - THAT/WHAT/WHICH 151

7. CHI - WHO 152

8. FUTURO - FUTURE 152

9. LAVARE/LAVARSI - TO WASH/TO CLEAN 152

10. CHIAMARE/CHIAMARSI - TO CALL/TO BE NAMED (MY NAME IS . . .) 153

11. ROMPERE/ROMPERSI - TO BREAK/TO BREAK A BONE OF YOUR BODY/TO BREAK DOWN 153

12. SBAGLIARE/SBAGLIARSI - TO MAKE A MISTAKE/ TO BE WRONG 154

13. ALZARE/ALZARSI - TO LIFT/TO WAKE UP/TO STAND UP 154

14. CHIEDERE/CHIEDERSI - TO ASK/TO WONDER 155

15. PIACERE- TO LIKE/NICE TO MEET YOU/PLEASURE/FAVOR 155

16. MOGLIE/MARITO- WIFE/HUSBAND 156
17. ZITTO - SILENT/SHUT UP 156
18. FEBBRE - FEVER/TEMPERATURE.. 156
19. IMPARARE - TO LEARN 156
20. UTILE/INUTILE - USEFUL/WORTHLESS 157
21. ESSERE/STARE - TO BE/TO STAY.. 157
22. SENTIRE/SENTIRCI - TO FEEL/TO HEAR 158
23. ANCHE/ANCORA - ALSO-TOO/STILL-AGAIN 158
24. FIORE - FLOWER 159
25. VIVERE/ABITARE - TO LIVE 159
26. VITA - LIFE/WAIST.. 159
27. MEZZO - MEDIUM/MEAN/HALF 160
28. ANTICO/VECCHIO - ANCIENT/OLD 161
29. ACCENDERE/SPEGNERE - TO SWITCH ON/TO SWITCH OFF 161
30. DOLCE/AMARO - SWEET/BITTER 161
31. C'È/CI SONO - THERE IS/ARE 161
32. POSSO/POTREI - CAN I/COULD I 162
EXCUSE ME, MAY I HAVE THE BILL? AND MAY I HAVE ONE
COFFEE AS WELL, PLEASE? 162
33. MADRE/PADRE-ZIA/ZIO-SORELLA/FRATELLO -
MOTHER/FATHER-AUNT/UNCLE-SISTER/BROTHER...................... 162
34. ANIMALE - ANIMAL... 162
35. MAI - EVER/NEVER.. 163
36. PIÙ . . . DI - MORE . . . THAN 163
37. MENO . . . DI - LESS . . . THAN 163
38. COME - AS . . . AS... 163
39. MIGLIORE - BETTER 163
40. PEGGIORE - WORSE 164
41. IL PIÙ - THE MOST 164
42. IL MIGLIORE - THE BEST 164
43. IL PEGGIORE - THE WORST 164
44. . . . ISSIMO/A - VERY... 164

45. IN/A – IN/TO	165
46. A – TO	165
47. DI – OF	165
48. DI/DA – FROM	166
49. CON – WITH/BY	166
50. SU – ON/OVER/ABOUT	166
51. FOR – PER	167
52. DA/PER – SINCE/FOR	167
53. CASO – CHANCE/CASE	168
54. CONOSCERE/SAPERE – TO KNOW/TO MEET	168
56. PERDERE – TO LOSE	169
57. ALLORA – THEN/SO/AT THE TIME	169
58. POI – THEN	170
59. FAR FARE QUALCOSA A QUALCUNO – TO MAKE SOMEBODY DOING	170
60. VOLARE – TO FLY	171
61. VICINO – NEAR/CLOSE/NEIGHBOR	171
62. TEMPO – TIME/WEATHER	172
63. SOTTOLINEARE – TO UNDERLINE/TO HIGHLIGHT	172
64. RICORDO – I REMEMBER/MEMORY /SOUVENIR	173
65. IL/LO – THE	173
66. I/GLI – THE	174
67. LA/LE – THE	174
68. UN/UNO – A/AN	175
69. UNA/UN' – A/AN	175
70. LUNGO/CORTO-BREVE – LONG/SHORT	176
71. ALTO/BASSO – TALL-HIGH/SHORT	176
72. PER DAVVERO-VERAMENTE/ATTUALMENTE – ACTUALLY/AT PRESENT/NOW	177
73. INFASTIDITO/ANNOIATO – ANNOYED/BORED	177
74. CORAGGIOSO/BRAVO IN/BRAVO A – BRAVE/GOOD AT	178

75. MACCHINA FOTOGRAFIA/CAMERA – CAMERA/ROOM/BEDROOM 178

76. RAGIONEVOLE/SENSIBILE/SENSITIVO – SENSIBLE/SENSITIVE/MEDIUM 179

77. FIDUCIA/CONFIDENZA – CONFIDENCE/FAMILIARITY 180

78. ESAURIENTE/COMPRENSIVO – COMPREHENSIVE/UNDERSTANDING/INCLUSIVE 180

79. MARCIAPIEDE/PAVIMENTO – PAVEMENT/FLOOR 181

80. COMODO/CONVENIENTE – COMFORTABLE/CONVENIENT/CHEAP 182

81. RIVISTA/MAGAZZINO – MAGAZINE/WAREHOUSE 182

82. GENITORE/PARENTE – PARENT/RELATIVE 183

83. ISTRUITO/EDUCATO – EDUCATED/POLITE 183

84. RENDERSI CONTO/REALIZZARE – TO REALIZE/TO CARRY OUT 184

85. ALLA FINE/EVENTUALMENTE – EVENTUALLY/IN CASE 184

86. ROMANZO/NOVELLA – NOVEL/SHORT STORY 185

87. BIBLIOTECA/LIBRERIA – LIBRARY/BOOKSHOP/BOOKCASE 185

88. DITTA/FIRMA – FIRM/SIGNATURE 186

89. PIATTO – DISH/FLAT 187

90. DOVERE – DUTY/MUST/TO HAVE TO 187

91. PASSATO – PAST/PASSED 188

92. REGALO – PRESENT/TO GIVE 188

93. ACCETTARE – TO AGREE TO/TO ACCEPT 189

94. NEVE/NEVICARE – SNOW/TO SNOW 189

95. PIOGGIA/PIOVERE – RAIN/TO RAIN 190

96. SALATO – SALTY/EXPENSIVE 190

97. OFFENDERE – OFFEND/TO HURT SOMEBODY'S FEELINGS 191

98. CI/NE – US/OURSELVES/TO US/THERE/ABOUT SOMETHING-SOMEONE/A CERTAIN QUANTITY OF SOMETHING-SOMEONE 192

99. MALE – BADLY/RUDELY/EVIL THINGS/EVIL 193

100. MALE – MOREOVER/FURTHERMORE 194

101. GAMBA – STRENGHT/COME ON! 194

102. FORZA - STRENGTH/COME ON! 195
103. IO FACCIO/TU FAI/LUI FA - I; YOU DO/ MAKE/ SHE DOES/MAKES 195
104. NOI FACCIAMO/LORO FANNO - WE; THEY DO/ MAKE 195
105. FATE - TO DO/MAKE/ FAIRIES 196
106. IO SO/TU SAI/LEI SA - I; YOU KNOW/SHE KNOWS 196
107. NOI SAPPIAMO/VOI SAPETE/LORO SANNO - WE; YOU; THEY KNOW 197
108. IO BEVO/TU BEVI/LUI BEVE - I; YOU DRINK/HE DRINKS 197
109. NOI BEVIAMO/VOI BEVETE/LORO BEVONO - WE; YOU; THEY DRINK 198
110. IO MI SIEDO/TU TI SIEDI/LEI SI SIEDE- I; YOU SIT DOWN/SHE SITS DOWN 198
111. NOI CI SEDIAMO/VOI VI SEDETE/LORO SI SIEDONO - WE; YOU; THEY SIT DOWN 199
112. IO STO/TU STAI/LUI STA- I; YOU STAY/HE STAYS 199
113. NOI STIAMO/VOI STATE/LORO STANNO - WE; YOU; THEY STAY 200
114. IO SCELGO/TU SCEGLI/LEI SCEGLIE- I; YOU CHOOSE/SHE CHOOSES 200
115. NOI SCEGLIAMO/VOI SCEGLIETE/LORO SCELGONO- WE; YOU; THEY CHOOSE 201
116. IO VENGO/TU VIENI/LUI VIENE- I; YOU COME/HE COMES 201
117. NOI VENIAMO/VOI VENITE/LORO VENGONO- WE; YOU; THEY COME 201
118. IO VADO/TU VAI/LEI VA- I; YOU GO/SHE GOES 202
119. NOI ANDIAMO/VOI ANDATE/LORO VANNO - WE; YOU; THEY GO 202
120. IO SALGO/TU SALI - I; YOU GO UP 203
121. VOI SALITE/LORO SALGONO - YOU; THEY GO UP 203
122. NOI SALIAMO - WE GO UP/WE SALT 203
123. SALE- SHE/HE GOES OUT/SALT 204
124. IO DICO/TU DICI/LUI DICE - I; YOU SAY/TELL/HE SAYS/TELLS 204

125. NOI DICIAMO/VOI DITE/LORO DICONO – WE; YOU; THEY SAY/TELL 205

126. IO ESCO/TU ESCI/LEI ESCE – I; YOU GO OUT/SHE GOES OUT .. 205

127. NOI USCIAMO/LORO ESCONO – WE; THEY GO OUT 206

128. USCITE – YOU GO OUT/EXITS 206

129. PROVA –TEST/PROOF/COMPETITION/ATTEMPT/REHEARSAL . 207

130. QUESTO/QUESTA/QUEST'– THIS 208

131. QUESTI/QUESTE – THESE 208

132. QUEL/QUELLO/QUELLA/QUELL' – THAT 209

133. QUEI/QUEGLI/QUELLE – THOSE 209

134. SÙBITO/SUBÌTO (CONSIDER THAT YOU WILL NOT FIND THE ACCENT GENERALLY, IT IS ONLY TO MAKE YOU UNDERSTAND THE DIFFERENT PRONUNCIATION) – RIGHT AWAY/IMMEDIATELY/SUFFERED/UNDERGONE 210

135. PRÌNCIPI/PRINCÌPI (CONSIDER THAT YOU WILL NOT FIND THE ACCENT GENERALLY, IT IS ONLY TO MAKE YOU UNDERSTAND THE DIFFERENT PRONUNCIATION) – PRINCES/BEGINNING/ORIGIN/FUNDAMENTALS/PRINCIPLES 211

136. PESCA (WITH A CLOSED SOUND OF THE "E")/PESCA (WITH AN OPEN SOUND OF THE "E" LIKE LUI È [HE IS])/ – FISHING/PEACH 212

137. FREDDO/CALDO – COLD/HOT/WARM 213

138. CHE/IL QUALE/LA QUALE/I QUALI/LE QUALI – WHO/WHOM/THAT/WHICH 214

139. DI CUI/DEL QUALE/DELLA QUALE/DEI QUALI/DELLE QUALI – WHOSE/OF WHICH/ABOUT WHICH 215

140. PER CUI/PER IL QUALE/PER LA QUALE/PER I QUALI/PER LE QUALI – SO/WHICH IS WHY/FOR WHICH 215

141. UOMO/DONNA/UOMINI/DONNE – MAN/WOMAN/MEN/WOMEN/HUMAN BEING 216

142. DATA/DATO – DATE/DATA/GIVEN/FACT/CERTAIN 217

143. SALTARE/SALPARE – TO JUMP/TO FAIL/ TO GO OUT/ TO SKIP/TO SET SAIL 217

144. PASTO/PASTA/PASTE – MEAL/PASTA/DOUGH/TEMPERAMENT/PASTRY 218

145. GIOCARE/GIOVARE – TO PLAY/TO IMPROVE/TO BENEFIT FROM 219

146. TESTO/TESTA/TESTE – TEXT/I TEST/HEAD/LEAD/WITNESS 220

147. ONORE/ONERE – REPUTATION/HONOR/PRIVILEGE/DUTY 220

148. GUARDARE/GUADARE – TO LOOK AT/TO WATCH/ TO CHECK/ TO FORD 221

149. SUPPORTARE/SOPPORTARE – TO PROP UP/TO SUPPORT/TO BEAR/TO STAND 222

150. DECIDERE/DECEDERE – TO DECIDE/TO DECEASE 223

151. VOLTA – TIME/VAULT 223

152. AMANTE – LOVER/ENTHUSIAST/LOVING 224

153. CHI – WHO 224

154. HOW – COME 224

155. DOVE – WHERE 225

157. PERCHÉ – WHY/BECAUSE 226

158. CHE COSA – WHAT 226

159. QUALE – WHAT/WHICH 226

160. QUANTO/QUANTA – HOW MUCH 226

161. QUANTI/QUANTE – HOW MANY 227

162. ESATTO – CORRECT/RIGHT 227

163. FALSO/SBAGLIATO – FALSE/LIE/FAKE/WRONG 228

164. VERO/GIUSTO/CORRETTO – REAL/TRUE/TRUTH/RIGHT/EXACT/FAIR/JUST 229

165. MANGIAVO/HO MANGIATO – I USED TO EAT/ I WAS EATING/ I ATE/I HAVE EATEN 230

166. ERA/È STATO – IT USED TO BE/ IT WAS/ IT HAS BEEN/AGE 231

167. SMETTERE – TO STOP/ TO QUIT/ TO GIVE UP 231

168. SPIEGARE – TO EXPLAIN/ TO UNFOLD/ TO DEPLOY/TO SPREAD 232

169. ARRESTARE – TO STOP/ TO ARREST 233

171. RAFFREDDORE/RAFFREDDARE – COLD/ TO COOL 234

172. PAESE – VILLAGE/ COUNTRY/NATION 234

173. MINUTO – MINUTE/ MOMENT/TINY/PUNY 235

174. GOLA – THROAT/ GLUTTONY/CANYON/GULCH 235

175. ECCO/ECO – HERE/ I SEE/THERE/OKAY 236

176. CERCARE – TO LOOK FOR/ TO SEEK/TO TRY 236

177. CELLULARE – CELL PHONE/ CELLULAR 237

178. FATTO – FACT/EVENT/DONE/MADE/BUILT 238

179. GRASSO – PLUMP/FATTY/FAT/OILY 238

180. INTELLIGENTE – BRIGHT/CLEVER 239

181. MACCHINA – CAR/MACHINE 240

182. NEGOZIO – SHOP/STORE 240

183. OGGI – TODAY/NOWADAYS 240

184. PARLARE – TO SPEAK/TO TALK/TO MAKE A SPEECH/TO CONFESS 241

185. RIPETERE – TO REPEAT/TO SAY SOMETHING AGAIN/TO KEEP HAPPENING 241

186. UFFICIO – OFFICE/DEPARTMENT 242

187. VIAGGIO – TRAVEL/TRIP/JOURNEY/I TRAVEL 242

188. IL BRACCIO/LE BRACCIA/I BRACCI – THE ARM/ THE ARMS 243

189. LA MANO/LE MANI – THE HAND/THE HANDS 244

190. IL DITO/LE DITA – THE FINGER/THE FINGERS 244

191. IL FINE/LA FINE – THE SCOPE/THE END 244

192. IL CAPITALE/LA CAPITALE – THE ASSETS/THE CAPITAL 245

193. IL CERO/LA CERA/C'ERO/C'ERA – CHURCH CANDLE/WAX/I WAS THERE/SHE WAS THERE/THERE WAS 245

194. PERDÒNO/PÈRDONO (CONSIDER THAT YOU WILL NOT FIND THE ACCENT GENERALLY; IT IS ONLY TO MAKE YOU UNDERSTAND THE DIFFERENT PRONUNCIATION) – I FORGIVE/FORGIVENESS/THEY LOSE 246

195. IL PIANTO/IO PIANTO/LA PIANTA – THE CRYING/THE PAIN/I PLANT/THE PLANT/THE DIAGRAM 247

196. PIANO/LA PIANA – FLAT/SLOW/QUIETLY/THE FLOOR/THE PLAN/PLAIN 247

197. IL METRO/LA METRO – THE METER/THE SUBWAY 248

198. IL ROSA/LA ROSA – THE PINK COLOR/THE ROSE 249

199. IL MODO/LA MODA - THE WAY/THE FASHION 249
200. IL PANNO/LA PANNA/I PANNI - THE CLOTH/THE CREAM/THE LAUNDRY 250
201. IL FRONTE/LA FRONTE - THE FRONT/THE FOREHEAD 250
202. IL POSTO/LA POSTA - THE SPACE/THE PLACE/THE MAIL/THE POST OFFICE 251
203. POTERE - ABILITY/POWER 251
204. ALMENO - AT LEAST/ IF ONLY 252
205. ANDATA - ONE WAY/FIRST LEG/SHE HAS GONE 252
206. CATTIVO - EVIL/NAUGHTY/NEGATIVE/TERRIBLE 253
207. DAMMELO/ME LO DIA PER FAVORE - GIVE IT TO ME!/GIVE IT TO ME PLEASE 254
208. FACCELO/CE LO FACCIA PER CORTESIA - LET US DOING SOMETHING/MAKE/DO IT TO US PLEASE 254
209. DIGLIELA/ GLIELO DICA PER FAVORE - TELL IT TO HIM/HER!/TELL IT TO HIM/HER PLEASE 255
210. VACCI/CI VADA PER FAVORE - GO YOURSELF/GO THERE PLEASE 255
211. STACCI/CI STIA PURE - STAY THERE IF YOU LIKE/YOU CAN STAY HERE IF YOU LIKE 256
212. SAPPI/SAPPIA - KNOW/PLEASE BE AWARE 256
213. ESSERE - BE/BE PLEASE 257
PLEASE, PROFESSOR, BE NICE WITH HIM; THE GUY HAS HAD SOME PROBLEMS RECENTLY, BUT HE IS TRYING TO SORT THEM OUT. 257
214. ABBI/ABBIA - BE/HAVE PLEASE 257
215. SETTIMANA/SETTIMA - WEEK/SEVENTH 257
216. SUCCESSO - SUCCESS/ACHIEVEMENT/APPROVAL/HAPPENED 258
217. TIPO - TYPE/MODEL/DUDE/CHARACTER 259
218. STORIA - HISTORY/STORY/MATTER/RELATIONSHIP/LIE 260
220. CASINO/CASINÒ - MESS/TROUBLE/CASINO 261
221. ACQUA/ACQUAZZONE - WATER/RAIN 262
222. RIPARTIRE - TO LEAVE AGAIN/TO TAKE OFF AGAIN/TO SHARE 262

223. CENTRO – CENTER/MIDDLE/DOWNTOWN 263
224. FOGLIO – SHEET OF PAPER/DOCUMENT/LAYER 264
225. GIORNO/GIORNATA – DAYTIME/DAY 264
226. TAGLIARE/RITAGLIARE – TO CUT/TO SLICE /TO CUT AGAIN/TO CUT OUT/TO SET ASIDE 265
227. GIACCA – JACKET/SUIT 266
228. SE TORNERAI-TORNI/ANDRÒ-VADO – IF YOU COME BACK/I WILL GO 267
229. SE AVESSI PIÙ DENARO/ANDREI – IF I HAD/I WOULD GO 267
230. SE AVESSE STUDIATO/AVREBBE SUPERATO – IF HE HAD STUDIED/HE WOULD HAVE PASSED 268
231. PAPÀ/PADRE/PAPA – DAD/FATHER/POP/FOREFATHER/FOUNDING FATHER 268
232. PRENDERE IN PRESTITO/PRESTARE – TO BORROW/TO LEND/TO SERVE 270
233. SEDERE/SEDERSI – TO SIT/TO BE SEATED/SOMEONE'S BEHIND 270
234. PRIMO/PRIMA – FIRST/FIRSTLY/EARLIER/IN THE PAST/SOONER/FIRST OF ALL/BEFORE/IN FRONT OF 271
CONCLUSION 273

Part 1: Italian for Beginners

A Comprehensive Guide for Learning the Italian Language Fast

Introduction

When a person decides to learn a new language, the reasons can vary—such as for business, tourism, and also "matters of love!" Thus, some of the advantages of learning a language deal with better work opportunities, traveling independently, reading a book or watching a movie in the original language, broadening personal relationships, etc. However, there isn't always a specific need. Sometimes people learn languages only to see the world from another point of view, or to train and stimulate the brain, improving creativity and problem-solving skills. For others, it could represent a hobby, similar to collecting things or playing a sport.

Languages are the reflection of a culture and country. Considering this, one can understand why many people want to learn Italian, even if it is a language that is spoken only in Italy. Its traditions and culture are what make Italian so fascinating. Its literature, art, music, food, and cities are all collected and reflected in the language and how it is expressed and used. Learning Italian means to get into the culture of the country, a place which is the result of the passage of many peoples, languages, and traditions. History has taught us that the culture which most influenced Italy, and so the Italian language, is the Roman one, whose roots are Latin. We also know that Romans spread their culture, language, and legal system almost everywhere. Due to this, there are many similarities between English and Italian, even if their linguistic family and origin are not the same. There are many Latin phrases used every day in English, such as "e.g", which stands for "exempli gratia", "for example", "etc."—which stands for "et cetera" and means "and so on". Or "i.e", which stands for "id est" that means "that is". These are Latin words but ones that are still used in English.

The process of learning a language is not easy and requires both a method and dedication. The purpose of this book is to show you that you can learn a language, no matter how hard it might seem in the beginning.

The first two parts of the book give you all the necessary tools to understand how to create a sentence and orient yourself in the depth of exceptions which characterized Italian as a Latin language.

In the third part, you will find dialogues with a step-by-step translation and some questions with answer keys. This section provides you with a practical use of the language in many common situations of daily life, so contextualizing all elements explained in the first two parts. Thus, dialogue represents a way to see how the Italian language works and helps you to understand it. One of the take-home messages of this book is that you need to express your thoughts to formulate questions and answer possible requests. Always keep in mind that you are learning another communication system, which can be similar to your native tongue, yet also different.

When dealing with a new language, you have to get the basic structure of a sentence. After which you will add new elements, new words (adverbs first, nouns, and adjectives). To start this process correctly, it is necessary to start with grammar, which represents the base of the language "tower". However, grammar is not enough; it is only with words that you have the "bricks" to build the "tower". For this reason, the last part of the book is dedicated to the glossary, which has been divided into basic verbs and nouns that relate to a given topic.

Good luck on your language learning journey!

Section 1 – Basis of Grammar

1.1 The Italian Alphabet: Spelling and Sounds

Italian is defined as a transparent language, which means that each letter corresponds to a sound—rather than in English, where each letter may correspond to many different sounds. This means that reading Italian is quite easy—you just have to follow some rules.

1.1.1 The Italian alphabet

Letters of the alphabet don't give pronunciation rules, but there are tools to spell out words:

A (**a** like the **a**rm)

B (**bi** like **bi**g)

C (**ci** like **ci**eat)

D (**di** like **di**slike)

E (**e** like **e**nd)

F (**effe** like **eff**ect)

G (**gi** like **gy**m)

H (**acca** like **acc**ount)

I (**i** like **i**mpress)

L (**elle** like **ele**ment with double l)

M (**emme** like **emme**r)

N (**enne** like **ene**rgy with double n)

O (**o** like **o**strich)

P (**pi** like **pi**g)

Q (**qu** like **qu**estion)

R (**erre** like **ere**ct with double r)

S (**esse** like **esse**ntial)

T (**ti** like **ti**p)

U (**u** like **pu**t)

V (**vu** like **wu**rst)

Z (**zeta** like **ze**st and **ta**p)

Remember: J, W, X, and Y don't exist in the Italian alphabet; if there are words with these letters, it means they are foreign words that have become part of the language.

While spelling, Italian people add the names of cities, as *A come Ancona* (A as Ancona), *B come Bologna* (B as Bologna), *C come Cagliari* (C as Cagliari), etc.

1.1.2 The Italian sounds

As mentioned, letters of the alphabet don't help so much with the pronunciation of letters, especially when they are combined.

1.1.2.1 Vowels

There are two types of vowel pronunciation in Italian: open and closed, and this literally depends on your mouth. Here are some examples:

A is always open and sounds like the a in the word f**a**st.

I is always closed and sounds like the double "ee" in English words, such as f**ee**t.

U is always closed as well, and it sounds like the double "oo" in English words, such as f**oo**t.

Instead, E and O can be both open or closed. The different use is linked to different Italian regions and dialects.

E is closed and sounds like the a in s**a**il, and when it is open, it sounds like the e in s**e**nd.

O is closed and sounds like the o in **o**pen, and when it is open, it sounds like the o in p**o**licy.

If you are thinking about how to recognize when they are open or not, don't worry. Time will help you, and also because the different use is linked to Italian regions and dialects. The most important difference, which is used in the same way for the whole country, is between È and E. The first one is open and corresponds to the English "is" (the third singular person of the verb to be - *essere*). It always has the stress to stand out from E, which means "and", and always has a closed sound.

1.1.2.2 Consonants

Most of the consonants sound as they are spelled, or read the same as in English. However, this does not happen with C, G, S, and Z.

The sounds of C and G depend on the vowel they come before, for example:

With E and I, the C sounds like the c in **ch**ase, while A, O, and U sound like the c in **c**astle.

With E and I, the G sounds like the g in **g**entle, while A, O, and U sounds like the g in **g**ap.

The sounds of S and Z depend on their position within the word, for example:

S sounds like the s in ri**s**e if it's in between two vowels, and like the s in **s**treet when it comes before a consonant

Z sounds like the ds in ad**ds** when the word starts with z; otherwise, it sounds like the ts in cu**ts**.

1.1.2.3 Combined sounds

The letters "c" and "g" change sound if they come before "h" and "s" before "c".

"ch" sounds like the "k" in **k**ey.

"gh" sounds like the "gu" in **gu**ilty.

"sc" sounds like the "sh" in **sh**ot.

There are also:

"gn" sounds like the "yo" in canyon.

"gl" sounds like the "lli" in mi**ll**ion.

1.2 Numbers, Days of the Week and Months

1.2.1 Numbers

To learn Italian numbers easily, you have to be careful while memorizing the ones that are completely different.

1.2.1.1 Cardinal Numbers

From zero to sixteen, they are completely different from each other.

0 zero

1 uno

2 due

3 tre

4 quattro

5 cinque

6 sei

7 sette

8 otto

9 nove

10 dieci

11 undici

12 dodici

13 tredici

14 quattordici

15 quindici

16 sedici

From seventeen to eighteen, you have to think about "dicia" as ten, plus the following number:

17 diciasette

18 diciotto

19 diciannove

Tens are:

20 venti

30 trenta

40 quaranta

50 cinquanta

60 sessanta

70 settanta

80 ottanta

90 novanta

If you want to say 21, 31, etc., and 28, 38, etc., you have to take off the final "a" and add "uno" or "otto". For example, ventuno or novantotto. For all the others, simply add the number after the ten. For example, trentadue, quarantatre, cinquantaquattro, sessantacinque, settantasei, ottantasette, etc.

You then have:

100 cento

1000 mille

It is simple going from one hundred, two hundred, three hundred, etc.; it is enough to add the number before "cento". For example, 500 is cinquecento (as the famous Italian car).

To go from one thousand, you do the same, but be careful: "mille" is used only for one thousand. In fact, from two thousand, you have to use "mila". For example, four thousand is quattromila.

1.2.1.2 Ordinal Numbers

From 1st to 10th, they are completely different from each other.

1st primo

2nd secondo

3rd terzo

4th quarto

5th quinto

6th sesto

7th settimo

8th ottavo

9th nono

10th decimo

From 11th, you simply add "esimo" at the end of the number by taking off its final vowel.

11th undicesimo

12th dodicesimo

13th tredicesimo

14th quattordicesimo

15th quindicesimo

20th ventesimo

and so on.

1.2.2 Days of the Week

The Italian days of the week come from Ancient Roman culture; "dì" stands for "day" and is another word for "giorno".

LUNEDÌ Monday

giorno della luna – day of the Moon

MARTEDÌ Tuesday

giorno di Marte – day of Mars

MERCOLEDÌ Wednesday

giorno di Mercurio – day of Mercury

GIOVEDÌ Thursday

giorno di Giove – day of Jupiter

VENERDÌ Friday

giorno di Venere – day of Venus

SABATO Saturday

giorno dei Saturno – day of Saturn

DOMENICA Sunday

giorno del Signore – day of Christ (from the Latin "Dominus")

All days can be plural, except Sunday, which is feminine, and they are all masculine (later, you'll see how to manage masculine and feminine, singular and plural).

1.2.3 Months

This is an easy part as they are very similar to the English ones.

GENNAIO January

FEBBRAIO February

MARZO March

APRILE April

MAGGIO May

GIUGNO June

LUGLIO July
AGOSTO August
SETTEMBRE September
NOVEMBRE November
DICEMBRE December

1.2.4 Dates

To express the date in Italian, it is not necessary to use first, second, third, etc. It works with one, two, three, etc. For example:

Today is September 23rd.

Oggi è il 23 di settembre.

Italians just use the cardinal number, plus "di", which means "of" and the month. The only exception is the first day of the month, where they use "primo" (first) too.

1.3 Articles

In Italian, as mentioned, names can be masculine or feminine. Gender can be recognized by the final vowel of the word ("o" for masculine and "a" for feminine), but there are also confusing cases, and so articles are the perfect tool to know if a word is masculine or feminine. Thus, a good way to learn words in Italian is to memorize words together with the corresponding article.

1.3.1 Definite articles

These are divided into masculine and feminine, and also into singular and plural. But the translation in English will be "the" for each one.

Masculine singular articles are: IL and LO.

Masculine plural articles are: I (for "il") and GLI (for "lo").

Feminine singular articles are: LA.

Feminine plural articles are: LE.

You might ask why there are two articles for masculine. This depends on how a word begins. If a word starts with "s" and a consonant, with "z", "gn", or a vowel, you have to use "lo". In this last case, "lo" loses its "o". In the spoken language, this will produce a sole sound, and in the written language, you will have to put an apostrophe instead of the "o"; for example, "lo albero" (the tree) will be "l'albero". The same will happen with feminine words starting with a vowel; for example, "la oca" (the goose) will be "l'oca".

The sole sound occurs only with singular names and articles, so "gli" and "le" won't ever lose their "i" and "e", and so the sound will be differentiated between the article and the name.

Their use has essential differences in English. First of all, Italian uses articles before a possessive (la mia casa, my home), and before the name of a continent, nation, and region, but not before a city. Another important difference is the use of the plural. In English, if you have to say that you like oranges, for example, you won't ever use "the oranges" if you are talking about oranges in general, not about specific ones. Instead, Italian will use it because names always come together with their articles.

1.3.2 Indefinite articles

These are divided into masculine and feminine, as definite ones, but they have only the singular form, like in English. The translation in English will be "a" or "an" for each one.

Masculine articles are: UN and UNO.

Feminine article is: UNA.

Again, you might wonder when to use "uno"; now the answer is easier: when you use "lo". As for definite articles, you will have a sole sound, and when the word that follows "uno" and "una" begins with a vowel—but only "una" will switch the "a" with the apostrophe; for example, "uno albero" (a tree) will be "un albero" and "una oca" (the goose) will be "un'oca".

1.4 Gender and Number

You are now ready to go deeper into how names and adjectives change, passing from masculine to feminine forms and vice-versa.

1.4.1 Gender

As previously stated, generally speaking, you can recognize if a word is masculine or feminine if it ends, in the singular, with "o" or "a". However, Italian also has words that end in "e". For this reason, it is crucial to learn words with their articles because it leaves no doubts about the gender.

The general rule identifies words with "o" as masculine and "a" as feminine; so, if you have to talk about a male cat, you will say "il gatto"; while you will say "la gatta" for a female cat.

Some names further change form when changing gender, as so in English, like:

il padre (the father)

la madre (the mother)

il marito (the husband

la moglie (the wife)

il fratello (the brother)

la sorella (the sister)

il toro (the bull)

la mucca (the cow)

Words that do not change are "il/la cantante" (the singer), "il/la parente" (the relative), and il/la nipote (nephew, niece, granddaughter, grandson). Words that change their meaning depending on the gender are "il porto" (the harbor), "la porta" (the door), "il fine" (the scope), and "la fine" (the end).

Furthermore, there are groups of words that belong to masculine or feminine. As mentioned, the days of the week are all masculine, except "domenica", but the names of trees, months, mountains, seas, rivers, and lakes are all masculine, too, while fruits, continents, states, regions, and islands are all feminine.

1.4.2 Number

If you have to transform a word from its singular to its plural form, you will have an easy job. In fact, all masculine words change their last vowel into an "i" and all feminine words into "e". For example, "il problema" will become "i problemi", and "la casa" will become "le case". All words ending in "e" will have an "i" at the end, and it doesn't matter if it is masculine or feminine— "l'informazione" will be "le informazioni" as "lo studente" will be "gli studenti". Moreover, words ending in "tà", usually feminine words, do not change; for example "la città" and "le città" (the city and the cities), as well as foreign words like "la foto" and "le foto" (the photo and the photos), "il video" and "i video", and "lo sport" and "gli sport". Don't forget the word "auto", which is a very common word used instead of "macchina", meaning "car".

When it comes to switching from singular to plural, there is also an aspect related to how their sounds change, too. As explained, "ch" makes the sound "k", and "gh" sounds like "gu" in guilty; this happens when it is together with "e" or "i". You also know that "c" sounds like "k" together with "a", "o", and "u" as you know that "g" sounds like "g" in garage. This means that you could have some problems while making the plural of words ending in "o", which is supposed to become "i" and ending in "a", which is then supposed to become an "e".

If you have to do the plural of a masculine word ending in "co", like "casco" (helmet), you have to consider that the "c" has the sound of "k"; thus, when you change the "o" with the "i" to make the plural, you will have to add an "h" to obtain the same sound because "ci" doesn't sound like "ki", but as "che" in cheap. For the same reason, with words ending in go, for the masculine plural, it is necessary to add an "h" after "g". If you have to do the feminine plural of words ending in "ca" or "ga", so when you have to switch the "a" with an "e", it will be the same. For example, "amica" (feminine friend) will be "amiche" (feminine friends) and "bottega" (small shop) will become "botteghe".

1.5 Prepositions

This topic is one of the most important of any language you want to learn. In fact, prepositions give roles to a word in a sentence. By using one of them, you give a particular meaning to that word depending on what you want to say. For example:

I am talking to you.

I am talking about you.

The sentence is the same except for "to" and "about". So, the first one uses "to" because it focuses on the person the narrator is talking to; the second one, "about", introduces the argument the narrator is talking about.

1.5.1 An overview of prepositions

As said, prepositions are a very important topic, but also complex. So, you will proceed step by step. Here is the list of Italian prepositions with a translation so that you have a general framework:

DI (of) - A (to) - DA (from) - IN (in) - CON (with) - SU (on, about) - PER (for) - FRA/TRA (between).

1.5.2 Prepositions and definite articles

The use of definite articles in Italian is different from English, especially because Italians use them everywhere. And, of course, they use them together with prepositions, too. When the prepositions "di", "a", "da", "in", and "su" come with a definite article, they become one word. Results of compositions are as follow:

DI+IL = del

DI+LO = dello

DI+LA = della

DI+I = dei
DI+GLI = degli
DI+LE = delle
A+IL = al
A+LO = allo
A+LA = alla
A+I = ai
A+GLI = agli
A+LE = alle
DA+IL = dal
DA+LO = dallo
DA+LA = dalla
DA+I = dai
DA+GLI = dagli
DA+LE = dalle
IN+IL = nel
IN+LO = nello
IN+LA = nella
IN+I = nei
IN+GLI = negli
IN+LE = nelle
SU+IL = sul
SU+LO = sullo
SU+LA = sulla
SU+I = sui
SU+GLI = sugli
SU+LE = sulle

It is not hard to use them; you just have to think.

1.5.3 Prepositions of time

These prepositions are used to introduce a time when something happened.

Use the preposition "a" with months (a marzo - in March), meals (a colazione - at breakfast, a pranzo - at lunch, a cena - at dinner), and periods (a Natale - at Christmas). To say the time, you have to use "a" again but together with the article (alle 5 - at 5 o'clock).

You use "in" with seasons (in estate - in summer) and with years, but plus the article (nel 1985 - in 1985).

Days do not need any preposition (lunedì - on Monday).

1.5.4 Prepositions of place

These prepositions refer to the position of something or someone.

Generally speaking, it is not so different from English; "a" translates "to" and is used for a movement toward a place, while "in" is used when inside a place. Some common verbs have a special use of the preposition, such as "stare" (to stay), which can be used both with "in" and "a", "partire" (to leave), which goes with "for", and "camminare" (to walk) that is followed by "verso" (towards), which is not a real preposition.

Things get more complicated with two verbs: "vivere" (to live) and "andare" (to go). If they are followed by cities, towns, villages, and small islands, the right preposition to use is "a". For example, "vado/vivo a Milano" - I go to Milan/in Milan. However, if continents, nations, regions, and big islands come after, you have to use "in". For example, "vado/vivo in Germania" - I go to Germany/in Germany.

1.6 Personal subject and direct pronouns

1.6.1 Personal subject pronouns

As in English, these work as a replacement of the subject, who does the action. Such as in the sentence, "Peter eats a piazza," the person who does the action is Peter, and he can be replaced by "he". Here is the Italian translation of personal subject pronouns:

IO = I

TU = YOU

LUI = HE

LEI = SHE

NOI = WE

VOI = YOU

LORO = THEY

As you can see, there is nothing to translate "it", and this is because Italians have a gender for things and animals, too, so they use "lui" for males and "lei" for females.

Moreover, remember that to be polite and formal, when speaking to a Mr (un signore) or a Mrs (una signora), Italian uses the 3rd singular person "lei" to refer both to a man or a woman.

So, "what's your name?" (informal) is: "come ti chiami?" and (formal) "come si chiama?"; "are you Mr. Rossi?" which is formal, is "Lei è il signor Rossi?"

1.6.2 Personal direct pronouns

As in English, they work as a replacement of the object, which is what undergoes the action. Such as in the sentence "Peter eats a pizza," the thing which undergoes the action is pizza, and it can be replaced by "it". Here are the Italian translations of personal direct pronouns:

MI = ME

TI = YOU

LO = HIM

LA = HER
CI = US
VI = YOU
LI = THEM (if referring to a "male" group)
LE = THEM (if referring to a "female" group)

This is only a direct translation of personal object pronouns. Later, their function in a sentence, together with other elements, is discussed. Right now, the only important thing to remember is that they always come before the verb.

1.7 Basic verbs: essere and avere

Essere (to be) and avere (to have) are the bases of each language and a good starting point for building sentences.

1.7.1. Essere

The use of essere is the same as "to be" in English, so it says more about people's appearances and professions, or an object's shape, color, size, etc.

IO SONO = I AM
TU SEI = YOU ARE
EGLI È = HE IS
ELLA È = SHE IS
ESSO/ESSA È = IT IS
NOI SIAMO = WE ARE
VOI SIETE = YOU ARE
ESSI/ESSE/LORO SONO = THEY ARE

Here, remember what was mentioned above regarding speaking Italian vowel sounds: "è" is the verb "to be" (corresponding to "is") and the sound is open, while "e" is a conjunction (corresponding to "and") and the sound is closed.

The expressions "there is" and "there are" are translated in Italian with "c'è" and "ci sono", where "c'" is the abbreviation of "ci", which means "there", "in that place".

1.7.2 Avere

The use of avere is the same as "to have" in English, so it refers to possessing something, someone (like relatives), and illnesses (like a headache).

IO HO = I HAVE

TU HAI = YOU HAVE

EGLI HA = HE HAS

ELLA HA = SHE HAS

ESSO/ESSA HA = IT HAS

NOI ABBIAMO = WE HAVE

VOI AVETE = YOU HAVE

ESSI/ESSE/LORO HANNO = THEY HAVE

Please note that the "h" in Italian does not have any sound; it is mute. So when speaking, there is no difference between "o" (or) and "ho" (I have) or "a" (to) and "ha" (has), or "anno" (year) and "hanno" (they have). However, when you write, you have to keep these differences in mind—even if it's one of the most common grammar mistakes (among Italians, too), people will understand you anyway.

1.7.3 Some different uses

Compared to English, there are some different uses of these two verbs.

1.7.3.1 Different uses of essere

These expressions, used in English with the verb "to be", are translated in Italian with "avere". You might find this strange; however, you just have to imagine that, if in English you would say,

"I'm cold," like you are feeling it, in Italian, you "possess" it, as when you say that you have got stomachache!

To be hungry = avere fame

To be thirsty = avere sete

To be sleepy = avere sonno

To be in a hurry = avere fretta

To be afraid = avere paura

To be hot = avere caldo

To be cold = avere freddo

To be right = avere ragione

To be wrong = avere torto

Note that, in English, these expressions are made by "to be" plus the adjective, while in Italian, by "avere" plus the noun.

1.7.3.2 Different uses of avere

These expressions, used in English with the verb "to have", are translated in Italian with "fare" (to do/to make). In this case, you just have to think that you are doing something. For example, in English, you say, "I have a shower," because you are referring to the act of "doing" it; in Italian, you exactly "do" it as when you say that you do your homework! Other expressions are simply translated with a specific verb.

To have breakfast = fare colazione

To have lunch = pranzare

To have dinner = cenare

To have a holiday = fare una vacanza

To have a nap = fare un pisolino

To have a shower/bath = fare una doccia/un bagno

To have a swim = fare una nuotata

To have a good time/fun = divertirsi

You still have to learn how to use verbs and how they change for each person and tense, so don't worry! Soon you will be able to use any Italian verb properly.

1.8 Demonstrative and possessive adjectives

Introducing these elements will give you the tools to build a sentence.

1.8.1 Demonstrative adjectives

The use of these is the same as in English. The only difference is that there is not only a singular and a plural form, but you also have to be careful with the gender.

This =   questo (for masculine) - questa (for feminine)

These = questi (for masculine) - queste (for feminine)

That = quel/quello (for masculine) - quella (for feminine)

Those = quei/quegli (for masculine) - quelle (for feminine)

As you can see, for that and those you have two forms for the masculine; it is not a problem, just follow the rules you have seen for articles. So, as you use "il", you will use "quel", and the use of "quello" is the same of "lo". Regarding rules about the apostrophe, use rules of the articles again both for "lo" and "la".

Keep in mind the English expression "what I see". For example, it is not translated in Italian with the corresponding word for "what"; you say "che cosa", but with "quello che vedo", where "che" is "that".

1.8.2 Possessive adjectives

When dealing with possessive adjectives, you focus on the person who has the "thing", and the person who owns it, like in English, but you also have to consider if the owned thing is masculine or feminine, and, of course, if it's singular or plural. However, remember that "his", "her", and "it" correspond to only one person, so one adjective. In this case, Italian does not make any difference. See below:

My = mio (masculine and singular), mia (feminine and singular), miei (masculine and plural), and mie (feminine and plural).

Your = tuo (masculine and singular), tua (feminine and singular), tuoi (masculine and plural), and tue (feminine and plural).

His/her/its= suo (masculine and singular), sua (feminine and singular), suoi (masculine and plural), and sue (feminine and plural).

Our = nostro (masculine and singular), nostra (feminine and singular), nostri (masculine and plural), and nostre (feminine and plural).

Your = vostro (masculine and singular), vostra (feminine and singular), vostri (masculine and plural), and vostre (feminine and plural).

Their = loro both for masculine and feminine, and both for singular and plural.

Here are some examples:

My dog = il mio cane (as "cane" is masculine).

My dogs = i miei cani.

His/her/its car = la sua macchina (as "macchina" is feminine).

Their house = la loro casa (as "macchina" is feminine).

Their houses = le loro case.

As you can see, every possessive adjective has the definite article beforehand; in Italian, it is mandatory, while in English, it's forbidden!

In Italian, it is not used when you speak about your family as a singular. For example: my brother will be "mio fratello", without the article. But my brothers will be "i miei fratelli", with the article.

1.9 Adverbs

In English, these are easy to recognize because they have the final part of the word in "ly" and they give further information about what is being done. If you say "you eat slowly," you want to say something more about eating. In Italian, "ly" is represented by "mente". Of course, to form an adverb, you have to start from the adjective, as in English. Here is how it works:

veloce (fast) = velocemente (fast) - in English, there is no difference between the adjective and the verb.

lento (slow) = lentamente (slowly).

regolare (regular) = regolarmente (regularly).

fortunato (lucky) = fortunatamente (luckily).

And so on. Please note that if the adjective ends with "e", making the adverbs it is lost, and if it ends in "o", it changes to "a".

Some adverbs do not come from an adjective, as in:

vicino (near), troppo (too/too much), là (there), qui (here), mai (ever/never), spesso (often), sempre (always), prima (before), and dopo (after).

1.10 Relative pronouns

These pronouns are used as in English, but in this case, Italian makes things a bit less complicated. In fact, there is no difference between objects and people; you will not have to think about whether the relative pronoun is replacing a thing or a person.

Before starting, you need to understand what a relative pronoun is:

The girl who is talking is my new classmate = In this sentence, WHO is the relative pronoun, and it works as the subject in the sentence "is talking", and it replaces "the girl".

The man (that) you saw yesterday is Peter's father = In this sentence, THAT is the relative pronoun, and it works as the object in the sentence "you saw" (you saw, who? the man...) and it replaces "the man".

Mark, whose brother attends your school, is coming to the party = In this sentence, WHOSE is the relative pronoun, and it works as "of who – possession" in the sentence "attends your school" and it replaces "the girl".

In the first and second cases, Italian uses CHE or QUALE. CHE never changes—it is always the same for masculine or feminine and singular or plural. Instead, QUALE never changes its form, but you have to put before it the correct definite article (IL for masculine singular; LA for feminine singular; I for masculine plural; LE for feminine plural; and LO and GLI are never used in this case).

In the last sentence, Italian uses QUALE again, but beforehand, you have to put DI plus the correct definite article, making the compound prepositions (DEL for masculine singular; DELLA for feminine singular; DEI for masculine plural; DELLE for feminine plural; and LO and GLI are never used in this case).

If you have to translate "to which", use QUALE again, but beforehand you have to put A plus the correct definite article, making the compound prepositions (AL for masculine singular; AL for feminine singular; AI for masculine plural; ALLE for feminine plural; and LO and GLI are never used in this case).

Please remember that the choice of the article depends on the gender and number of the replaced word. For example, "alla quale" = "to which" referring "to her", "ai quali" = "to which" referring "to them" (all males), etc. Of course, the same can be used with other prepositions, and this depends on what you want to say. For example, "for which" = per il/la/i/le quali, "on which" = sul/sulla/sui/sulle quali, etc.

There is another option that works without the article and only with the preposition, CUI. As it can be used only with prepositions, it will never replace the subject or object. For example: "whose" = del/della/dei/delle quali or DI CUI, "to which" = al/alla/ai/alle quali or A CUI, and so on.

1.11 Demonstrative and possessive pronouns

There is no difference between demonstrative and possessive adjectives and pronouns. Of course, pronouns come without a name after...

This is my laptop, that is yours.

Questo è il mio computer portatile, quello è tuo.

As you can see, "tuo" is a pronoun and it is perfectly the same as the adjective.

1.12 Interrogative pronouns

These pronouns are used to make questions, as in English. The only difference is that, in Italian, the preposition comes before the interrogative pronoun and not at the end of the sentence:

Where are you from?

Di dove sei?

First of all, note that "from" is translated with "di" and not "da". This is because to speak about the place of origin, Italian uses "di". Afterward, you can see that the preposition is before "dove" (where) and not at the end of the question.

Other interrogative pronouns are:

CHI = who

COME = how

QUANDO = when

PERCHÉ = why/because (there is no difference in Italian)

QUANTO/A = how much

QUANTI/E = how many

QUALE = what/which

CHE COSA/CHE = what

1.13 Indefinite adjectives and pronouns

Indefinite adjectives and pronouns are used to indicate a certain quantity of something or number of people or to refer to something or someone which is not determined.

1.13.1 Indefinite adjectives

To indicate a certain quantity, a non-specific number of something or people, English uses some, any, and no. Now, see their translations in Italian through some examples:

There are some oranges in the fridge - where "some" is the indefinite adjective.

In Italian, there are several ways to translate "some"; in this case, like "alcune", "delle", and "qualche", but you have to observe that "oranges" is a countable name, which is technically a name that can have a plural form. So, the translation will be:

Ci sono alcune/delle/arance in frigo - C'è qualche arancia in frigo.

In the sentence, "there is some sugar". The word sugar is uncountable (so it has only the singular form) and so the Italian translations for some are "un po'" (which is the abbreviation of "un poco" - a little) or "dello". So, the translation will be:

C'è un po'/dello zucchero.

To sum up, with the singular, you can use "un po'", "del/dello/della"; and with the plural, "alcuni/alcune", "dei/degli/delle" (according to the gender and the number of the noun they refer to), and qualche (which doesn't ever change and goes always with a singular name). These indefinite adjectives are the same when used in questions. A difference you may remember is that, usually, Italian doesn't use them in a negative sentence, so there is no translation for "any" or "no" when you want to say there is no quantity of what you are talking about.

For example, if you take the previous two examples and turn them into the negative form, you will have:

There are no oranges in the fridge/there aren't any oranges in the fridge - Non ci sono arance.

There is no sugar/there isn't any sugar - Non c'è zucchero.

As you can see, there is no indefinite adjective.

If you want to translate "no" not to speak about quantity, but to say "at all", you can use "nessuno" or "nessuna", and remember that the masculine form loses the final "o". For example:

Non c'è nessuno problema - there is no problem (at all).

Non c'è nessuna soluzione - there is no solution (at all).

1.13.2 Indefinite pronouns

These pronouns in English are simply obtained by putting together "some", "any", and "no" with "thing" or "body"/"one" when they refer to people. In Italian, these pronouns have different forms and different uses, actually quite complicated ones—but don't worry; it is possible to learn them focusing on their translation. Some of them change according to gender and number, others only regarding the number, and others never change. Now you will go through them one by one.

Alcuno, alcuna, alcuni and alcune.

As you can see, this changes according to the gender and number; it refers both to things and people, and it translates "somebody"/"something" in the affirmative sentences, and "anybody"/"anything" or "nobody"/"nothing in the negative ones. But remember: It can work also as an adjective as you have already seen. An example:

Alcuni sono al mare oggi - Somebody is at the beach today.

C'è qualche problema? No, nessuno - Is there any problem? No, nothing.

Qualcuno, qualcuna, qualcuni and qualcune.

These also change according to the gender and number; they refer both to things and people, and it translates "somebody"/"something" in the affirmative sentences, and "anybody"/"anything" in the interrogative ones. It only works as a pronoun:

C'è qualcuno in casa? Si, c'è Maria - Is there anybody home? Yes, there is Maria.

È notte, e c'è qualcuno alla scuola. È strano - It's night, and there's someone at school. It's weird.

Nessuno, nessuna

These can be only masculine or feminine, and it translates "anybody"/"anything" or "nobody"/"nothing in the negative sentences. It can also work as an adjective, as you have already seen.

Non c'è nessuno a casa - There is nobody at home/there isn't anybody at home.

Lastly, there are indefinite pronouns, which have only one form for both masculine and feminine and singular and plural and are used for things. These are "qualcosa" and "niente".

C'è qualcosa da bere? No, non c'è niente - Is there anything to drink? No, there is nothing/there isn't anything.

Please note that "niente" has a negative value, but in Italian, you always have to use "non" to make the negative form of the verb too.

Other forms are:

"ciascuno" and "ciascuna", that don't have the plural form and translates "each one" or "each ones"; "ognuno" and "ognuna", that don't have the plural form too and are used to translate "everything" or "everybody"; and "chiunque" that only has one form and is used for people to translate "anybody" when, in English, it is used in affirmative sentences. The correspondent form of "anything" used in the same case will be "qualsiasi cosa".

Lui ama chiunque - He loves anybody.

Lui ama qualsiasi cosa - He loves anything.

There are other forms, but the above is enough for now, as this is all you need to start speaking Italian!

1.14 Quantifiers

You have seen how to express an indefinite quantity, but you still need to learn how to express a big or small amount of something. In English, there are many ways to say it, so now see translations starting from English. Before starting, consider that what is uncountable in English, is the same in Italian, except for:

advice (consiglio), accommodation (alloggio), furniture (mobile), information (informazione), news, (notizia) and hair (capello).

All of these words have a plural form in Italian.

Poco and poca - little (used for what you can't count).

Pochi and poche - few (used for what you can count).

Molto/tanto and molta/tanta - much (used for what you can't count).

Molti/tanti and molte/tante - many (used for what you can count).

Troppo and troppa - too much (used for what you can't count).

Troppi and troppe - too many (used for what you can count).

Of course, in addition, it is not possible to count singular forms with words, and with plural forms, which are possible to count, you always have to pay attention to the gender of the name that follows.

For example, if you want to say "there is too much sugar in this cake and few apples," you have to consider that sugar is uncountable, while apples are countable. Furthermore, "sugar" is "zucchero", which is a masculine singular word, and "apples" is "mele", a feminine plural word.

The translation will be:

C'è troppo zucchero in questa torta e poche mele.

1.15 Comparatives and superlatives

1.15.1 Comparatives

As in English, comparatives are used to compare two elements with an adjective in order to say that one element is as, less, or more than the other one.

1.15.1.1 Comparative of equality

This uses the word "come" - as - after the adjective:

"Mario è alto come Luca" - Mario is as tall as Luca.

1.15.1.2 Comparative of minority

This uses the word "meno" - less - before the adjective and "di" after it (which stands for "than" in English):

"Mario è meno alto di Luca" - Mario is less tall than Luca.

1.15.1.3 Comparative of majority

This uses the word "più" - more - before the adjective and "di" after it (which stands for "than" in English):

"Mario è più alto di Luca" - Mario is taller than Luca.

Also, in Italian, "buono"- good - and "bad" - cattivo - are irregular.

buono - migliore.

cattivo - peggiore.

1.15.2 Superlatives

As in English, superlatives are used to compare a small unit to a group. In Italian, they are formed by adding the definite article before the adjective:

"Mario è il più alto della classe" - Mario is the tallest of the class.

"Laura è la meno simpatica delle sorelle" - Laura is the less nice of the sisters.

"Nicola è il migliore, e Paolo il peggiore" - Nicola is the best, and Paolo is the worst.

Section 2 – Verbal System

Before going through all the moods and tenses of Italian verbs, you have to focus on the three conjugations that represent the basic elements to get the pattern of each declension.

The moods are: indicativo, condizionale, congiuntivo, and imperativo. In this book, you won't learn about congiuntivo, which is the most complicated one, as it is studied at a higher level.

Italian has three conjugations: ARE, ERE, and IRE. Verbs with these endings are the infinitive forms—what English expresses by TO plus the base form of the verb. What makes these three conjugations different are the vowels A, E, and I before "re"; these vowels characterize the verbs in each mood and tense.

2.1 Present tenses

There are two present tenses in Italian used in the indicative mood: "presente indicativo" and "stare" plus "gerundio". To link them to a general translation in English, you can think that "presente indicativo" corresponds to "present simple" and "stare" plus "gerundio" is the "present continuous" where "stare" is the verb "to be" and gerundio is the "ing form". The way they are used in Italian is a bit different, but you will start from their construction.

2.1.1 Presente indicativo

Just like English, in Italian, you have to start from the infinitive form; if English takes "to" off before the verb and adds subjects in its place, Italian removes "are", "ere", and "ire" and changes them with an ending that is different for each person (and this is why it is not necessary to use the subject before the verb). Start from the first conjugation, taking "amare" - to love as an example:

Io AMO, tu AMI, egli/ella AMA, noi AMIAMO, voi AMATE, loro AMANO.

As you can observe, the vowel "a" tags this first conjugation (except for "io" and "tu"), and the first part of the verb "am" never changes.

Now see how it works with the second and third conjugation, which are alike.

"scrivere" - to write:

Io SCRIVO, tu SCRIVI, egli/ella SCRIVE, noi SCRIVIAMO, voi SCRIVETE, loro SCRIVONO.

"partire" - to leave:

Io PARTO, tu PARTI, egli/ella PARTE, noi PARTIAMO, voi PARTITE, loro PARTONO.

As you can note, the vowels "e" and "o" tag the second and the third conjugation (except for "tu" and "noi", which is the same for all conjugations), and the first part of the verbs "scriv" and "part" never change.

As you have seen for the plural form, you have to think again about sounds; if you take a verb ending in "care" or "gare", you will see that with the person "tu", you have to make some changes to maintain the sound. For example:

the verb "giocare" - to play - cannot be "tu gioci" because this will be the sound of the "c" in "church" and it is not the same as the "c" in giocare, which sounds like the "c" in "castle". For this reason, you should add an "h" after the "c" and it will be "tu giochi".

Unfortunately, there are many irregular verbs. Below are the most common ones:

"andare" - to go

Io VADO, tu VAI, egli/ella VA, noi ANDIAMO, voi ANDATE, loro VANNO

"bere" - to drink

Io BEVO, tu BEVI, egli/ella BEVE, noi BEVIAMO, voi BEVETE, loro BEVONO

"dare" - to give

Io DO, tu DAI, egli/ella DÀ, noi DIAMO, voi DATE, loro DANNO

"dire" - to say/to tell

Io DICO, tu DICI, egli/ella DICE, noi DICIAMO, voi DITE, loro DICONO

"fare" - to do

Io FACCIO, tu FAI, egli/ella FA, noi FACCIAMO, voi FATE, loro FANNO

"salire" - to go/come up

Io SALGO, tu SALI, egli/ella SALE, noi SALIAMO, voi SALITE, loro SALGONO

"sapere" - to know

Io SO, tu SAI, egli/ella SA, noi SAPPIAMO, voi SAPETE, loro SANNO

"uscire" - to go out

Io ESCO, tu ESCI, egli/ella ESCE, noi USCIAMO, voi USCITE, loro ESCONO

"venire" - to come

Io VENGO, tu VIENI, egli/ella VIENE, noi VENIAMO, voi VENITE, loro VENGONO

2.1.2 Stare plus gerundio

As this is made of two parts, you have to understand how they are formed. First of all, see the presente indicativo di "stare", which is irregular:

"stare" – to stay

Io STO, tu STAI, egli/ella STA, noi STIAMO, voi STATE, loro STANNO.

Gerundio is formed by adding "ando" for verbs in ARE, and "endo" for verbs in ERE and IRE to the fixed part of the verb.

amare – amando

scrivere – scrivendo

partire – partendo

2.1.3 How to use "presente indicativo" and "stare plus gerundio"

When introducing these tenses, a translation was given, and it was stated that the use is a bit different. Now, you will see how.

"Stare plus gerundio" is only used when you have to speak about something that is happening at the moment, right now. Be careful— never use it for future actions; that is presente indicativo's job.

In fact, if you want to say, "I am having dinner with some friends tonight," you will have to say, "Ceno con alcuni amici stasera," and not "sto cenando." If the phrase is, "I am having dinner with some friends now," – "Sto cenando con alcuni amici ora," you will have two options. Sometimes, you can use the presente indicativo instead of "stare plus gerundio," but still to refer to something is happening now. For example: "Che cosa fai?" -- "Sto leggendo un libro"; this will be translated as "What are you doing?" – "I'm reading a book". But you could also use the form "che cosa stai facendo". In this case, it does not matter.

2.1.4 Adverbs of frequency

When the presente indicativo is used to speak about a habit in the present, as the present simple does in English, you may need adverbs of frequency that are words that indicate how something is done:

Always - sempre

Often - spesso

Usually - solitamente/di solito

Sometimes - qualche volta

Once - una volta

Twice - due volte (and so on)

Ever/never - mai

2.2 Past tenses

There are several past tenses in Italian: some belong to the indicative and others to other moods. Don't worry—you are not going to learn all of them here, but to begin, you will start with the indicative mood.

2.2.1 Passato prossimo

This is the most used tense to speak about the past, and so it's something you need to learn. Technically, you could compare it with the present perfect (I have gone, you have eaten, etc.), but its form and use is very different and the translation also corresponds to the past simple.

Firstly, you have to focus on the main difference: in English, you always use the verb "to have" to form compound tenses, while in Italian, you can use both "avere" and "essere" for the present indicativo. It sounds complicated, but it isn't. To understand what verbs go with "avere" and which ones go with "essere", you have to start from the concept of transitive and intransitive verbs—strange words but with easy practical meanings. Basically, a transitive verb is a verb that has an object, something that answers the questions "who" or "what"; for example, in the sentences "Mary called Lucy" or "Mary made a cake," Mary is the subject, so she is making the action, and "Lucy" and "cake" are the objects as they answer the question "who" for "Lucy" and "what" for "a cake". On the contrary, intransitive verbs do not have an object; for example, in the sentence "Mary went to the park," nothing answers the questions "who" or "what", because "in the park" better answers the question of "where".

So, transitive verbs are compound with "avere", while intransitive verbs are compounded with "essere". Here are some example sentences:

Mary called/has called Lucy - Mary ha chiamato Lucy

Mary made/has made a cake - Mary ha fatto una torta

but Mary went/has gone to the park - Mary è andata al parco

Unfortunately, there are many intransitive verbs, which use "avere" instead of "essere". The most common are:

Camminare - to walk, viaggiare - to travel, lavorare - to work, cenare - to have dinner, piangere - to cry, dormire - to sleep - etc.

As you can see, after "avere" and "essere", there are "chiamato", "fatto", and "andata"; these are past participles, which in English, when regular, are formed by adding "ed" at the end of the verb.

In Italian, regular past participles are formed by adding ATO for verbs in ARE, UTO for verbs in ERE, and ITO for verbs in IRE to the fixed part of the verb:

"andare" becomes "andato"

"credere" becomes "creduto"

"dormire" becomes "dormito".

There is only one problem—many verbs have an irregular past participle. The most common are:

"to open": aprire - aperto

"to drink": bere – bevuto

"to ask": chiedere – chiesto

"to close": chiudere – chiuso

"to run": correre – corso

"to say/tell": dire – detto

"to be": essere – stato

"to do/make": fare – fatto

"to read": leggere – letto

"to put": mettere – messo

"to die": morire – morto

"to be born": nascere – nato

"to lose": perdere – perso

"to take": prendere – preso

"to answer": rispondere – risposto

"to break": rompere – rotto

"to chose": scegliere – scelto

"to get down": scendere – sceso

"to write": scrivere – scritto

"to switch off": spegnere – spento

"to spend": spendere – speso

"to happen": succedere – successo

"to see/watch": vedere – visto

"to come": venire – venuto

"to won": vincere – vinto

"to live": vivere – vissuto

When there are lists of irregular verbs, it is common to think "No way!" but consider that many of the verbs above are irregular in

English, too! So, just keep calm and try to learn them two by two or try to form phrases with them and take your time.

There is something more to know about the past participle in Italian. In fact, if you observe the example above, you can see that the past participle changes depending on the person whom it is referring to:

"Mary ha fatto una torta" but "Mary è andata al parco", where "fatto" ends with "o" and "andata" with "a". This is because when you use verb "essere" to make compound forms of the verbs, the past participle takes the number and gender of the person who is making the action, the subject; this never happens when you use "avere" to make compound tenses. So:

"Io ho/tu hai/egli/ella ha/noi abbiamo/voi avete/loro hanno FATTO una torta."

"Io sono/tu sei/egli/ella è ANDATO-ANDATA al parco."

"Noi siamo/voi siete/loro sono ANDATI-ANDATE al parco."

2.2.2 Imperfetto

This tense does not exist in English, so it is not possible to give a translation; you will see later how to use past tenses in Italian compared to English. For the moment, just learn how to form it.

As for the presente indicativo or past participle, you always have to take the fixed part of the verb:

"to go": andare – io andavo, tu andavi, egli/ella andava, noi andavamo, voi andavate, loro andavano.

"to spend": spendere – io spendevo, tu spendevi, egli/ella spendeva, noi spendevamo, voi spendevate, loro spendevano.

"to leave": partire – io partivo, tu partivi, egli/ella partiva, noi partivamo, voi partivate, loro partivano.

As you can see, the fixed part of the verb never changes but also the final parts "vo", "vi", va", "vamo", "vate", and "vano"; the only thing that changes is the vowel between the fixed part of the verb (called the root) and the ending part of it (called the suffix). So, you have "a" for verbs in "are", "e" for verbs in "ere", and "i" for verbs in "ire". Easy, isn't it? So, to make it a bit harder, here are the irregular verbs:

"to be": essere - io ero, tu eri, egli/ella era, noi eravamo, voi eravate, loro erano.

"to do/make": fare - io facevo, tu facevi, egli/ella faceva, noi facevamo, voi facevate, loro facevano.

"to say/tell": dire - io dicevo, tu dicevi, egli/ella diceva, noi dicevamo, voi dicevate, loro dicevano.

"to drink": bere - io bevevo, tu bevevi, egli/ella beveva, noi bevevamo, voi bevevate, loro bevevano.

To learn them easier and faster, note that the only thing which changes is the root of the verb, the fixed part, except for "essere": "fare" becomes "fac-", "dire" becomes "dic-", and "bere" becomes "bev-".

The expressions "there was" and "there were" are translated in Italian with "c'era" and "c'erano", where "c'" is the abbreviation of "ci", which means "there", "in that place".

2.2.3 Stare plus gerundio

Now a quick look at the past version of "stare" plus gerundio. The form is the same seen for the present, except, of course, for the tense of "stare", which is used at the imperfetto:

Io STAVO, tu STAVI, egli/ella STAVA, noi STAVAMO, voi STAVATE, loro STAVANO plus amando, scrivendo or partendo. The translation corresponds to the past continuous:

Luca stava mangiando una pizza - Luca was eating a pizza.

2.2.4 Uses of passato prossimo, imperfetto, and stare plus gerundio

Before going through the uses of passato prossimo, imperfetto, and stare plus gerundio, it is important to know that there is another past tense called "passato remoto" that corresponds to the English past simple, but you won't study it for the moment. This tense is not used in the colloquial language, except for some regions in the south of Italy and Tuscany. For this reason, you can use passato prossimo when referring to a concluded action in the past or an action that is something that has just finished and somehow still has connections with the present, but is over. You can also use passato prossimo to speak about what happened once or never.

Here are some examples:

Ieri sono andato al parco - Yesterday I went to the park (concluded action in the past).

Ho appena finito di mangiare - I have just finished eating (just concluded action).

Non sono mai stato a Londra - I have never been to London (something that never happened).

On the other hand, if the action in the past describes a habit in the past, something you used to do, imperfetto is the right tense. However, it is also used to describe an ongoing action in the past (where English would use past continuous), to speak about a certain state, description of a state of mind, or of how something or someone appeared, and when an action represents the cause of something else when it has a consequence.

Here are some examples:

Mentre Mary studiava, Peter leggeva - While Mary was studying, Peter was reading (two ongoing actions in the past).

Faceva freddo, ed io ero molto felice perché nevicava - It was cold, and I was happy because it was snowing (two descriptions - "was cold" and "was happy" - and one ongoing action in the past - "was snowing").

Ieri Mary aveva la febbre e così non è andata al lavoro - Yesterday Mary had a fever and so she didn't go to work ("aveva la febbre" is the reason whe she "didn't go to work").

As you can see, only ongoing actions are translated with the past continuous in English; the rest use the past simple. So, if you have to translate a past simple or present perfect from English to Italian, stop and think: if it is a description, a habit in the past, or an action that caused something else, use imperfetto!

As you have just seen, with an ongoing action, you use imperfetto, but you can use also the imperfetto of "stare" plus gerundio, which is the perfect correspondent of the past continuous in English. Take the previous example, where imperfetto expressed an ongoing action:

Mentre Mary studiava, Peter leggeva – While Mary was studying, Peter was reading.

In this sentence, there are two verbs at imperfetto, and both represent ongoing actions in the past; so, the sentence could also be, "Mentre Mary stava studiando, Peter stava leggendo".

The same for "nevicava in the following sentence: "Faceva freddo ed io ero molto felice perché nevicava" – It was cold and I was happy because it was snowing – could be "faceva freddo ed io ero molto felice perché stava nevicando". To sum up, if you need to express an ongoing action, which took place in the past, and that, in English, would use the past continuous, in Italian, you have two options: imperfetto and imperfetto of "stare" plus gerundio.

<u>2.2.5 Past expressions and adverbs</u>

As stated, passato prossimo translates both the past simple and present perfect; therefore, you can have it with:

Last – scorso/passato

Ago – fa

When – quando

While – mentre

Ever/never – mai

Just – appena

Already – già

Yet – ancora (only negative)

Lately – recentemente

So far – finora

There are also two prepositions associated in English with the present perfect: since and for. In this case, Italian does not use any past tenses, but the presente indicativo. For example:

In the sentence "I have known him since 2000/we were children/for 20 years," you don't have to use any past tense in Italian, only the present: "Lo conosco dal 2000/da quando eravamo bambini/ da 20 anni." As you can see, both "since" and "for" are translated with the preposition "da" followed by "quando". If there is a verb introducing the past expression, "I have known" is "conosco", which is presente indicativo.

2.2.6 Trapassato prossimo

The name of this tense sounds scary, but it is not too complicated. Firstly, you have to know that it corresponds to the English past perfect, and, both in English and Italian, it is used to refer to an action that happened before another in the past. For example:

I had just ended my essay when I got the email and had to do another one. I was so sad!

Here, the action of "ending" happens before "getting the email".

To make this tense in Italian, consider that it is quite similar to passato prossimo, but it does not use the presente indicativo of "essere" or "avere". Now see the translation of the phrase above:

Avevo appena finito il mio saggio quando ho ricevuto una email e dovevo farne un altro. Ero così triste!

Here, "avevo appena finito" corresponds to "I had just ended", and it is trapassato prossimo.

2.3 Reflexive and indirect personal pronouns

2.3.1. Reflexive pronouns

These are: MI – myself, TI – yourself, SI – herself/himself/itself, CI – ourselves, VI – yourselves, and SI – themselves.

Their use is strictly linked to reflexive verbs.

2.3.2 Reflexive verbs

These are verbs whose meaning depends on the presence of reflexive pronouns. In fact, some of them have a meaning with the reflexive pronouns, but have a different one without it, while others only work with the reflexive pronoun. When a verb comes together with a reflexive pronoun, the latter comes before the verb. Here is an example:

lavarsi – to wash oneself

io mi lavo, tu ti lavi, egli/ella si lava, noi ci laviamo, voi vi lavate, loro si lavano

Of course, the tense of the verb changes based on the context.

There are four types of reflexive verbs:

1. The ones, like "lavarsi", where who is doing the action is doing it to himself/herself;

2. Verbs where who is doing the action isn't doing it to himself/herself, but to something that belongs to him. For example, "lavarsi i denti" – to brush "your" teeth;

3. Verbs where those people who are doing the action do so to each other, like "salurarsi" – to greet, noi ci salutiamo – we say goodbye (literally – I greet you, and you greet me).

4. The ones that only work as reflexive but do not have a reflexive meaning, like "arrabbiarsi": io mi arrabbio – I get mad.

There are many verbs belonging to group 1, and these change meaning, as stated before, if they come with or without a reflexive pronoun. Here is the list:

Alzare – to lift/alzarsi – to get up

Cambiare - to change/cambiarsi - to change clothes

Chiamare - to call/chiamarsi - to be named

Rompere - to break/rompersi - to break your bones.

Sbagliare - to make a mistake/sbagliarsi - to get wrong

2.3.3 Indirect personal pronouns

In Section 1, you saw direct personal pronouns—the ones that replace the object. Now you will see indirect personal pronouns, used in other cases—when a preposition precedes them. For example:

I do it for you - we came with her - they are speaking about him

Here "you", "her", and "him" are indirect personal pronouns because they come after a preposition. Before going on, note that even "him" in this sentence: "I told him" is an indirect personal pronoun because it works as it was "to him".

The following pronouns always come after a preposition:

me - te - lui - lei - noi - voi - loro.

I do it for you: "Lo faccio per te" (where "it" and "lo" are direct personal pronouns); we came with her: "Noi veniamo con lei"; they are speaking about him: "Loro stanno parlando di lui".

With the preposition "to", so "a", there two options:

I told him: "Io parlo a lui" - "Io gli parlo".

So, it is possible to use "a" plus the indirect personal pronouns you have seen to work after the preposition, or:

mi - ti - gli (a lui) - le (a lei) - ci - vi - gli

and they always come before the verb and do not use any preposition. See all the examples below:

You give me an advice: "Mi dai un consiglio".

I give you an advice: "Ti do un consiglio".

I give him an advice: "Gli do un consiglio".

I give her an advice: "Le do un consiglio".

You give us an advice: "Ci dai un consiglio".

I give you an advice: "Vi do un consiglio".

I give them an advice: "Gli do un consiglio".

2.3.4 Combined personal pronouns

Now, see what happens when you have to use both a direct personal pronoun and an indirect one.

In the sentence "I'm writing a letter to Mary," "a letter" is the object and "to Mary" is to whom; if you have to replace them with a personal pronoun, you will have: "it" and "to her", and the sentence will become: "I'm writing it to her."

In Italian: "Sto scrivendo una lettera a Maria."

Starting from the object "una lettera", you will have to use the direct personal pronoun "la" (as "lettera" is feminine and singular).

"La sto scrivendo a Maria."

Then, replace only "a Maria" using the indirect personal pronoun "le" (a lei - to her).

"Le sto scrivendo una lettera."

However, when you have to use them together, the indirect personal pronoun will go before the direct personal pronoun and will change their form becoming:

me - te - glie (both for "gli" and "le") - ce - ve - glie and the example sentence: "Sto scrivendo una lettera a Maria" becomes: "Gliela sto scrivendo."

Only "glie" becomes one word with the direct personal pronoun because the others keep being alone:

Lui sta scrivendo una lettera a me - He's writing a letter to me - me la sta scrivendo.

Io sto scrivendo una lettera a te - I'm writing a letter to you - te la sto scrivendo.

Io sto scrivendo una lettera a lui/a lei" - I'm writing a letter to him/to her - gliela sto scrivendo.

Lei sta scrivendo una lettera a noi - She's writing a letter to us - ce la sta scrivendo.

Io sto scrivendo una lettera a voi - I'm writing a letter to you - ve la sto scrivendo.

Io sto scrivendo una lettera a loro - I'm writing a letter to them - gliela sto scrivendo.

The last thing you have to know deals with personal pronouns and compound tenses. As stated, the past participle never changes with avere; this is not completely true as it changes when, with direct or combined personal pronouns, taking the gender and number of the direct pronoun. For example:

"Ho portato la macchina a Luca" - Gliel'ho portata, where "portata" agrees with "l'", which stands for "la" and refers to "macchina".

2.3.5 Verb "piacere"

This verb translates "to like", and if the meaning is the same, English and Italian build it in a very different way.

In English, the subject of "like" is the person who likes something or someone; in Italian, the subject is what is liked, and to understand who likes it, you have to say whom that thing or person is liked by specifically. It sounds like a turn of phrase, but look at the examples below:

I like chocolate - so "chocolate" is what is liked, and "I" represents who likes it. In Italian, the translation of this sentence is "mi piace la cioccolata," where "cioccolata" is the subject of the verb "piace" and "mi" stands for "to me". Another example:

She likes oranges - le piacciono le arance, where "arance" is the subject of the verb "piacciono" and "le" stands for "to her".

So, if the thing or person liked is singular, you have to use "piace"; if plural, it is "piacciono".

2.4 Imperative

The imperative is used to express orders to someone and usually to "you"; corresponding forms of "you" in Italian are "tu" (singular) and "voi" (plural).

"Tu" uses the 3rd person singular of presente indicative for verbs in ARE; "voi" uses the 2nd person plural of presente indicative:

mangiare –

magia! (tu)

mangiate! (voi)

While for verbs in ERE and IRE both "tu" and "voi" use the correspondent forms of presente indicativo, so the 2nd singular and plural persons:

spendere –

spendi! (tu)

spendete! (voi)

dormire -

dormi! (tu)

dormite! (voi)

There is another form of imperative that sounds more as an invitation, which is used in English with "let's" plus the verb. This, in Italian, corresponds to the 1st person plural of the presente indicativo:

andiamo! (noi) – let's go!

There are also forms to refer formally to Mr and Mrs, so "lei", but you won't see them this time because they use the congiuntivo, which you will study in upper levels.

However, there is still something you have to know about the imperativo; the position of personal pronouns in this mood.

In the sentence "tu scrivi una lettera a Maria," you know that "lettera" corresponds to the direct personal pronoun "la", and "a Maria" to the indirect personal pronoun "le"; you also know that together they become "gliela". In all moods, these pronouns come before the verbs, except the imperativo and infinito.

gliela scrivi (presente inidicativo)

scrivigliela! (imperativo)

scrivergliela (infinito)

2.5 Future

2.5.1 Simple future

The use of this tense corresponds to the English "will" plus verb; as stated, the present continuous with a future value, in Italian, is given by the presente indicativo. Now see how to form it.

All verbs add "erò" for "io", "erai" for "tu", "erà" for "lui/lei", "eremo" for "noi", "erete" for "voi", and "eranno" for "loro":

io amerò, scriverò, partirò

tu amerai, scriverai, partirai

lui/lei amerà, scriverà, partirà

noi ameremo, scriveremo, partiremo

voi amerete, scriverete, partirete

loro, ameranno, scriveranno, partiranno

Until now nothing particularly hard.

However, there are verbs whose fixed part changes; otherwise, their sound will be weird:

"andare" (to go) becomes andr-

"avere" (to have) becomes avr-

"dovere" (to have to) becomes dovr-

"potere" (can) becomes potr-

"sapere" (to know) becomes sapr-

"vedere" (to see/to watch) becomes vedr-

"vivere" (to live) becomes vivr-

"bere" (to drink) becomes berr-

"tenere" (to keep) becomes terr-

"venire" (to come) becomes verr-

2.5.2 Compound future

As passato prossimo, this tense is compound, and so you will have to use the future simple of avere, for transitive verbs, and of essere, for intransitive verbs, plus the past participle. For example:

avrò, avrai, avrà, avremo, avrete, avranno mangiato

sarò, sarai, sarà andato/andata – saremo, sarete, saranno andati/andate

The use of "futuro composto", this is its name in Italian, is the same as "will" plus "have" plus "past participle" in English: When she will have arrived, I will cook the dinner.

It is used to speak about an action that will happen before another one in the future.

Actually, in Italian, there is another use, which expresses a supposition about something that could have happened. For example:

"Mary è in ritardo, avrà perso il treno." – "Mary is late; she would have missed the train."

2.6 Conditional

There are only two tenses here: present and past. The present corresponds to the English "would" plus "base form", "could", "may/might", and the past to "would/could/may/might have" plus "past participle". Both in English and Italian, the conditional is used formally or to express a possibility.

2.6.1 Present conditional

All verbs add "erei" for "io", "eresti" for "tu", "erebbe" for "lui/lei", "eremmo" for "noi", "ereste" for "voi", and "erebbero" for "loro":

io amerei, scriverei, partirei

tu ameresti, scriveresti, partiresti

lui/lei amerebbe, scriverebbe, partirebbe

noi ameremmo, scriveremmo, partiremmo

voi amereste, scrivereste, partireste

loro, amerebbero, scriverebbero, partirebbero

As you can see, it is very similar to the simple future; in fact, the verbs that change the fixed part of the future, do the same with the conditional.

Be careful! The 1st person plural "noi" differs from the simple future to the present conditional for one "m":

noi ameremo, scriveremo, partiremo - simple future

noi ameremmo, scriveremmo, partiremmo - present conditional

2.6.2 Past conditional

As all compound tenses, the past conditional also uses the present conditional of "avere" for transitive verbs, and "essere" for intransitive verbs, plus the past participle. For example:

avrei, avresti, avrebbe, avremmo, avreste, avrebbero mangiato

sarei, saresti, sarebbe andato/andata - saremmo, sareste, sarebbero andati/andate

2.7 Modal verbs: potere, volere, e dovere

These verbs are used in a language to determine the intention of an action: "potere" is used to ask or give permission, "volere" to express an intention or a desire or to speak about a possibility, and "dovere" for an obligation. If another verb follows, it has to be the infinitive form:

"posso aprire la finestra?" - can I open the window?

"voglio leggere" – I want to read

"devo lavorare" – I must/have to work

2.7.1 Potere

2.7.1.1 Presente indicativo

CAN – TO BE ABLE TO

Io posso, tu puoi, lui/lei può, noi possiamo, voi potete, loro possono

2.7.1.2 Passato prossimo e imperfetto

COULD – WAS/WERE – HAVE/HAS BEEN ABLE TO

Io ho, tu hai, lui/lei ha, noi abbiamo, voi avere, loro hanno potuto

Io potevo, tu potevi, lui/lei poteva, noi potevamo, voi potevate, loro potevano

2.7.1.3 Gerundio

BEING ABLE TO

potendo

HAVING BEEN ABLE TO

avendo potuto

2.7.1.4 Future

WILL BE ABLE TO

Io potrò, tu potrai, egli/ella potrà, noi potremo, voi potrete, loro potranno

WILL HAVE BEEN ABLE TO

Io avrò, tu avrai, egli/ella avrà, noi avremo, voi avrete, loro avranno potuto

2.7.1.5 Conditional

COULD – WOULD BE ABLE TO – MAY – MIGHT

Io potrei, tu potresti, egli/ella potrebbe, noi potremmo, voi potreste, loro potrebbero

WOULD HAVE BEEN ABLE TO

Io avrei, tu avresti, egli/ella avrebbe, noi avremmo, voi avreste, loro avrebbero potuto

2.7.2 Volere

2.7.2.1 Presente indicativo

TO WANT

Io voglio, tu vuoi, egli/ella vuole, noi vogliamo, voi volete, loro vogliono

2.7.2.2 Passato prossimo e imperfetto

WANTED -HAVE/HAS WANTED

Io ho, tu hai, egli/ella ha, noi abbiamo, voi avere, loro hanno voluto

Io volevo, tu volevi, egli/ella voleva, noi volevamo, voi volevate, loro volevano

2.7.2.3 Gerundio

(it is not used in English)

volendo

(it is not used in English)

avendo voluto

2.7.2.4 Future

WILL WANT

Io vorrò, tu vorrai, egli/ella vorrà, noi vorremo, voi vorrete, loro vorranno

WILL HAVE WANTED

Io avrò, tu avrai, egli/ella avrà, noi avremo, voi avrete, loro avranno voluto

2.7.2.5 Conditional

WOULD LIKE TO

Io vorrei, tu vorresti, egli/ella vorrebbe, noi vorremmo, voi vorreste, loro vorrebbero

WOULD HAVE LIKED TO

Io avrei, tu avresti, egli/ella avrebbe, noi avremmo, voi avreste, loro avrebbero voluto

2.7.3 Dovere

2.7.3.1 Presente indicativo

MUST - TO HAVE TO

Io devo, tu devi, egli/ella deve, noi dobbiamo, voi dovete, loro devono

2.7.3.2 Passato prossimo e imperfetto

HAD TO - HAVE/HAS TO

Io ho, tu hai, egli/ella ha, noi abbiamo, voi avere, loro hanno dovuto

Io dovevo, tu dovevi, egli/ella doveva, noi dovevamo, voi dovevate, loro dovevano

2.7.3.3 Gerundio

HAVING TO

dovendo

HAVING HAD TO

avendo dovuto

2.7.3.4 Future

WILL HAVE TO

Io dovrò, tu dovrai, egli/ella dovrà, noi dovremo, voi dovrete, loro dovranno

WILL HAVE TO

Io avrò, tu avrai, egli/ella avrà, noi avremo, voi avrete, loro avranno dovuto

2.7.3.5 Conditional

WOULD HAVE TO

Io dovrei, tu dovresti, egli/ella dovrebbe, noi dovremmo, voi dovreste, loro dovrebbero

WOULD HAVE HAD TO

Io avrei, tu avresti, egli/ella avrebbe, noi avremmo, voi avreste, loro avrebbero dovuto

2.8 CI and NE

Italian is the language of tiny words; in a sentence, you can hear many small words. In the previous part, you saw direct and indirect personal pronouns and how they can be combined, but there are two other small words, which are often used both in the common and formal language: "ci" and "ne".

2.8.1 Ci

You have already met this word; it can be a reflexive personal pronoun for "noi", a direct personal pronoun for "noi", or an indirect personal pronoun instead of "noi":

"Noi ci chiamiamo Marco e Marta." - Our names are Marco and Marta.

"Chi ci porta alla stazione?" - Who is taking us to the station?

"Ci piace il gelato" - We like ice cream.

However, sometimes it does not refer to "noi" but to "where", working as "there", in English, when you don't want to repeat the name of a place. Here are some examples:

"Hai mai visitato Siena?" - Have you ever visited Siena?

"Si, ci sono stato lo scorso anno." - Yes, I have. I was there last year.

Here "ci" stands for "Siena", and "ci" as a pronoun with a verb that is not imperative or infinitive, is placed before it.

"Sei stato al cinema di recente?" - Have you been to the cinema recently?

"No, non ci vado da molto tempo, ma vorrei andarci." - No, I haven't. I haven't gone (there) in a long time, but I would like to go (there).

In this sentence, both instances of "ci" stand for "cinema"; the first one comes with a verb at passato prossimo, and so it is before the verb, while the second one is together with the verb essere, at the end - "andare" is the infinitive. You can also see how Italian always uses "ci" even when English tends to imply it.

In fact, when speaking about "verbo essere" and "imperfetto", you have seen that the expressions "there is/there was" and "there are/there were" are translated in Italian with "c'è/c'era" and "ci sono/c'erano", where "c'" is the abbreviation of the "ci" currently being referenced.

<u>2.8.2 Ne</u>

This Italian word is frequently used and replaces "of something or someone". At first, it might seem complicated, but after reviewing some examples, the meaning will be clear:

"Buongiorno, Signora Rossi, quante mele vuole?" - Good morning, Mrs. Rossi, how many apples would you like?

"Buongiorno, ne vorrei dieci." - I would like ten (of apples), please.

"Che cosa è successo a Roma? Ne parlano da giorni." - What happened in Rome? They have been talking about it for days.

In the first sentence, "ne" replaces "apples", so "of them"–that English doesn't use–, while in the second sentence, it stands for "che cosa è successo", what happened, "about it".

Do you remember that mi, ti, gli/le, ci, vi, and gli change their form when they come together with a direct personal pronoun, becoming me, te, glie, ce, ve, and glie? The same happens when they come together with "ne". For example:

"Hai parlato del viaggio a Paolo?" - Have you talked to Paolo about the trip?

"Si, gliene ho parlato ieri sera." - Yes, I have. I talked to him (about it) last night.

Here, "glie" replaces "Paolo" (to him), and "ne" replaces "about the travel" (which English doesn't repeat).

2.8.3 Ci and Ne together

When "ci" comes together with "ne", it becomes "ce":

"quante palle ci sono nella scatola?" - How many balls are there inside the box?

"ce ne sono venti" - There are twenty (of balls, which is "ne" in Italian).

In this case, "ci" replaces "nella scatola" and becomes "ce" because it comes together with "ne".

"C'è del burro in frigo?" - Is there any butter in the fridge?

"No, non ce n'è." - No, there isn't any.

Here, again, "ci" replaces "nel frigo" and becomes "ce" because it comes together with "ne", which in turn loses the final "e" because of "è" after.

Section 3 – Grammar Exercises

This section is dedicated to some grammar exercises that will be very useful for you to test yourself on the topics learned in Sections 1 and 2.

3.1 Articles, gender, and number

<u>3.1.1 Fill in the gaps with the correct definite or indefinite article:</u>

    a)   A che ora arriva_____autobus?

What time does the bus arrive?

    b)   _____mattina di solito lavoro.

Usually, I work in the morning.

    c)   Paolo parla con_____suoi amici.

Paolo is speaking with his friends.

    d)   Manuele è_____studente diligente.

Manuel is a diligent student.

    e)   La Sig.ra Rossi è_____nostra insegnante di matematica

Mrs. Rossi is our Maths teacher.

    f)   _____problema è che non ho molti soldi, è _____periodo difficile.

The problem is that I don't have much money; it is a hard period.

 g) Questo è_____esercizio molto facile.

This exercise is very easy.

 h) Ho_____amica che vive a Londra.

I have got a friend who lives in London.

 i) Domani ho_____esame di italiano.

Tomorrow, I have an/the Italian exam

j) _____libro di matematica è costoso.

This Maths book is very expensive.

3.1.2 Transform the following sentences into the plural form:

 a) Il libro è interessante.

The book is interesting.

 b) L'amica è felice.

The friend is happy.

 c) La tazza di tè è sul tavolo.

The teacup is on the table.

 d) La porta è chiusa.

The door is closed.

 e) Il gioco nuovo è nella scatola.

The new game/toy is inside the box.

 f) L'amico di Paolo è al lavoro.

Paolo's friend is at work.

 g) La sorella di Marta è molto bella.

Marta's sister is very beautiful.

 h) Lo studente è intelligente.

The student is smart.

i) La città è affollata.

The city is crowded.

j) Il bar è chiuso.

The bar is closed.

3.2 Subject and direct pronouns

3.2.1. Substitute the underlined words with the correct subject pronoun or find the implicit subject:

a) <u>Maria</u> canta sempre quando cucina. _____

Maria always sings while she cooks.

b) <u>Carlo e Anna</u> lavorano nello stesso ufficio. _____

Carlo and Anna work in the same office.

c) <u>Mi piace</u> molto la carne ma <u>preferisco</u> il pesce. _____

I like meat a lot, but I prefer fish.

d) <u>Il tavolo</u> è marrone. _____

The table is brown.

e) <u>Mia sorella ed io</u> viviamo con i nostri genitori. _____

My sister and I live with our parents.

f) <u>Luca</u> non conosce mio fratello. _____

Luca doesn't know my brother.

g) <u>Andate</u> spesso al cinema. _____

You often go to the cinema.

h) <u>Sono</u> tutti italiani in questo bar. _____

They are all Italian in this bar.

i) <u>Chi</u> ha già visto questo film? _____

Who has already watched this movie?

j) <u>Il gatto</u> di Marco si chiama Paolo, come mio padre. _____

Marco's cat name is Paolo, like my father.

3.2.2. Substitute the underlined words with the correct object pronoun, then write the sentence again:

a) La professoressa spiega <u>la lezione</u> agli studenti.

The professor explains the lesson to the students.

b) Oggi al mercato compro <u>le mele</u>.

Today, I am buying apples at the market.

c) Avete già spedito <u>gli inviti</u> per la festa?

Have you already sent the invitations to the party?

d) Ieri ho conosciuto <u>le nuove amiche di mia sorella</u>.

Yesterday, I met my sister's new friends.

e) Federico ha comprato <u>i biglietti</u> per il concerto.

Federico has bought the tickets for the concert.

f) Tua zia non scrive mai <u>lettere</u>.

Your aunt does not ever write letters.

g) Non capisco perché Paolo chiama sempre <u>me</u>.

I do not understand why Paolo always calls me.

h) Ieri ho visto <u>tuo cugino</u> alla fermata dell'autobus.

Yesterday, I saw your cousin at the bus stop.

i) Ho già invitato <u>te</u>.

I have already invited you.

j) Non vogliamo offendere <u>voi</u>.

We do not want to offend you.

3.3 Prepositions and verbs essere and avere

3.3.1 Fill in the gaps choosing the correct option:

a) Viaggio spesso 1. _____ lavoro perché 2. _____un agente 3. _____commercio. Mi vesto sempre elegante,4. _____la giacca.

I often travel for work because I am a salesman. I always dress up in a suit.

1. a) per, b) di, c) sul

2. a) siete, b) sei, c) sono

3. a) per, b) di, c) nel

4. a) alla, b) con, c) della

    b) Amo viaggiare perché posso prendermi una pausa 1. _____impegni d'ufficio. 2. _____Brasile ci vado ogni anno; mi piace camminare 3. _____strade piene 4. _____colori e gente.

I love traveling because I can take a break from office duties. I go to Brazil every year; I like walking through colored and crowded streets.

1. a) sulle, b) dagli, c) degli

2. a) in, b) per, c) a

3. a) per, b) sulle, c) nella

4. a) nel, b) a, c) di

    c) Mi sono trasferita 1. _____Italia 2. _____amore e ora 3. _____ a Roma 4. _____fare un corso di italiano.

I moved to Italy for love and now I am in Rome to attend an Italian course.

1. a) a, b) nell', c) in

2. a) all', b) di, c) per

3. a) siamo, b) è, c) sono

4. a) del, b) per, c) a

    d) 1. _____due fratelli e una sorella; Maria invece 2. _____solo un fratello e 3. _____molto simili.

I have got two brothers and one sister; Maria, instead, has only got one brother and they are very similar.

    e) 1. a) ho, b) abbiamo, c) avete

f) 2. a) ha, b) hai, c) hanno

g) 3. a) siamo, b) sono, c) siete

h) Noi oggi 1. _____ delle cose da fare 2. _____centro; vieni 3. _____noi? C' 4. _____anche Giovanna.

Today, we have some things to do downtown; are you coming with us? Giovanna is coming too.

1. a) ho, b) abbiamo, c) avete

2. a) al, b) per, c) in

3. a) di, b) nel, c) con

4. a) è, b) ha, c) sono

3.4 Demonstratives and possessive adejectives

3.4.1 Fill in the gaps with the correct demonstrative adjective:

a) _____qui davanti è casa mia, _____in fondo alla strada è di mia sorella.

This is my house; the one at the end of the street is my sister's.

b) Non mi piace _____dolce.

I do not like this dessert.

c) Chi è_____ragazza seduta laggiù?

Who is that girl over there?

d) Ragazzi, _____qui è il mio amico Gianni.

Guys, this is my friend Gianni.

e) _____arco è l'Arco di Costantino.

This/that is Constantine's Arch.

f) Metto le scarpe da ginnastica o_____qui con il tacco?

Shall I wear tennis shoes or these high-heeled shoes?

g) _____è il mio libro di italiano, _____sul tavolo è il vostro.

This Italian book is mine; that one on the table is yours.

h) _____sono i miei genitori, Mario e Lucia.

These are my parents, Mario and Lucia.

i) _____ è il volo per Milano.

This is the flight to Milan.

j) In_____classe dove siamo noi c'è la lezione di storia, _____studenti laggiù vanno alla lezione di filosofia.

In this class, where we are, there is a history class; those students over there are going to the philosophy class.

<u>3.4.2 Fill in the gaps with the correct possessive adjective or pronoun:</u>

a) Piero ci ha invitati a cena a casa_____.

Piero has invited us for dinner at his place.

b) Mi piace la_____borsa; dove l'hai presa?

I like your purse; where did you get it?

c) I_____genitori sono andati al cinema con _____fratello più piccolo.

My parents have gone to the cinema with my younger brother.

d) I_____amici mi aiutano sempre.

My friends always help me.

e) Ragazze, dove sono le_____amiche?

Girls, where are your friends?

f) La_____cultura è molto interessante perché siamo un popolo antico.

Our culture is very interesting because we are an ancient population.

g) Bambini, chi sono i_____genitori?

Kids, who are your parents?

h) La_____fortuna è stata che vi abbiamo incontrati.

Your luck was that we met you.

i) Mario e Susanna hanno cambiato macchina, la_____era molto vecchia.

Mario and Susanna changed car; theirs was very old.

  j) Devo chiamare Giulia e dirle che la_____macchina è pronta.

I have to call Giulia and tell her that her car is ready.

3.5 Presente indicativo

3.5.1 Fill in the gaps with the correct form of the 1st person singular of the presente indicativo of verbs in brackets:

  Ciao, 1. _____(chiamarsi) Thomas e 2. _____(essere) di Cracovia, ma 3. _____(abitare) a Roma da qualche mese. Per adesso 4. _____(vivere) in albergo ma 5. _____(cercare) casa. Da un po' di tempo 6. _____(guardare) gli annunci online ma non 7. _____(trovare) nulla di interessante. Domani 8. _____(andare) in agenzia e 9. _____(sperare) di trovare una persona che mi aiuti. 10. _____(avere) molta fiducia.

Hi, my name is Thomas, and I am from Cracow, but I have been living in Rome for a few months. By now, I am living in a hotel, but I am looking for a flat. For a while, I have been looking at real estate ads online, but I am not finding anything interesting. Tomorrow, I am going to a real estate agency, and I hope to find a person who can help me. I have a lot of faith.

3.4.2 Fill in the gaps with the correct form of the 3rd person singular of the presente indicativo of verbs in brackets:

  Lui 1. _____(chiamarsi) Thomas e 2. _____(essere) di Cracovia, ma 3. _____(abitare) a Roma da qualche mese. Per adesso 4. _____(vivere)in albergo ma 5. _____(cercare) casa. Da un po' di tempo 6. _____(guardare) gli annunci online ma non 7. _____(trovare) nulla di interessante. Domani 8.

_____(andare) in agenzia e 9. _____(sperare) di trovare una persona che lo aiuti. 10. _____(avere) molta fiducia.

He is Thomas, and he is from Cracow, but he has been living in Rome for a few months. By now, he is living in a hotel, but he is looking for a flat. For a while, he has been looking at real estate ads online, but he is not finding anything interesting. Tomorrow, he is going to a real estate agency, and he hopes to find a person who can help him. He has a lot of faith.

3.6 Past tenses

3.6.1 Fill in the gaps with the correct form of the passato prossimo or imperfetto of verbs in brackets:

Un pappagallo 1. _____(scappare) di casa: 2. _____(succedere) qualche giorno fa a Milano. I proprietari 3. _____(essere) molto tristi ma 4. _____(raccontare) la storia del pappagallo ai giornali. 5._____(chiamarsi) Ugo e per loro 6. _____ (essere) come un figlio. Lo 7. _____(lasciare) sempre libero in casa, ma un giorno il vento 8. _____(aprire) la finestra e lui 9. _____(volare) via. Fortunatamente lo 10. _____(trovare) pochi giorni dopo grazie all'aiuto di molti cittadini.

A parrot ran away from home: it happened some days ago in Milan. The owners were really sad, but they told the story of the parrot to the newspapers. Its name was Ugo, and it was like a son to them. They always let it fly free inside the house, but one day the wind opened the window, and it flew away. Luckily, they found it a few days after thanks to the help of many citizens.

3.7 Combined personal pronouns

3.7.1 Fill in the gaps with the correct combined personal pronoun:

a) Porto alla nonna la torta - _____porto.

I am taking the cake to Grandmother.

b) Ci scrivi il tuo indirizzo? - _____scrivi?

Can you write us your address?

c) Per Natale regalo un viaggio a Mario - _____regalo per Natale.

For Christmas, I want to give a trip to Mario.

d) Chi vi presta la macchina per il viaggio? - _____presta?

Who is going to lend you the car for the trip?

e) Hanno scritto un messaggio ai loro amici - _____hanno scritto.

They have written a message to their friends/they have texted their friends.

f) Mi spieghi l'esercizio perché non l'ho capito? - _____spieghi che non l'ho capito?

Can you explain to me the exercise because I did not understand it?

g) Avete chiesto a Paola se voleva venire anche lei? - _____avete chiesto?

Have you already asked Paola if she wants to come as well?

h) Ti hanno già consegnato il pacco? - _____hanno già consegnato?

Have they already delivered you the parcel?

i) Avete comprato i cioccolatini al nonno? - _____avete comprati?

Have you already bought pralines for Grandfather?

j) Ho regalato una collana alla mia fidanzata - _____ho regalata.

I gave my girlfriend a necklace as a gift.

3.8 Articles, gender, and number

3.8.1 Fill in the gaps with the correct definite or indefinite article:

a) A che ora arriva **l'**autobus?

b) **La** mattina di solito lavoro.

c) Paolo parla con **i** suoi amici.

d) Manuele è **uno** studente diligente.

e) La Sig.ra Rossi è **la** nostra insegnante di matematica

f) **Il** problema è che non ho molti soldi, è **un** periodo difficile.

g) Questo è **un** esercizio molto facile.

h) Ho **un'**amica che vive a Londra.

i) Domani ho **l'/un** esame di italiano.

j) **Il/un** libro di matematica è costoso.

3.8.2 Transform the following sentences into the plural form:

a) Il libro è interessante. **I libri sono interessanti**

Books are interesting

b) L'amica è felice. **Le amiche sono felici**

Friends are happy

c) La tazza di tè è sul tavolo. **Le tazze di tè sono sui tavoli**

Teacups are on the tables

d) La porta è chiusa. **Le porte sono chiuse**

Doors are closed

e) Il gioco nuovo è nella scatola. **I giochi nuovi sono nelle scatole**

New games/toys are inside the boxes

f) L'amico di Paolo è al lavoro. **Gli amici di Paolo sono al lavoro**

Paolo's friends are at work

g) La sorella di Marta è molto bella. **Le sorelle di Marta sono molto belle**

Marta's sisters are very beautiful

h) Lo studente è intelligente. **Gli studenti sono intelligenti**

Students are smart

i) La città è affollata. **Le città sono affollate**

Cities are crowded

j) Il bar è chiuso. **I bar sono chiusi**

Bars are closed

3.9 Subject and direct pronouns

3.9.1. Substitute the underlined words with the correct subject pronoun or find the implicit subject:

a) Maria canta sempre quando cucina. **Lei**

She

b) Carlo e Anna lavorano nello stesso ufficio. **Loro**

They

c) Mi piace molto la carne ma preferisco il pesce. **Io**

I

d) Il tavolo è marrone. **Esso**

It

e) Mia sorella ed io viviamo con i nostri genitori. **Noi**

We

f) Luca non conosce mio fratello. **Lui**

He

g) Andate spesso al cinema. **Voi**

You

h) Sono tutti italiani in questo bar. **Loro**

They

 i) <u>Chi </u>ha già visto questo film? **Lui/lei**

He/she

 j) <u>Il gatto</u> di Marco si chiama Paolo come mio padre. **Lui**

He (but, in English, "it" because it refers to a cat)

3.9.2. Substitute the underlined words with the correct object pronoun, then write the sentence again:

 a) La professoressa **la** spiega agli studenti.

 b) Oggi al mercato **le** compro.

 c) **Li** avete già **spediti** per la festa?

 d) Ieri **le** ho conosciut**e**.

 e) Federico **li** ha comprat**i** per il concerto.

 f) Tua zia non **le** scrive mai.

 g) Non capisco perché Paolo **mi** chiama sempre.

 h) Ieri **l'**ho visto alla fermata dell'autobus.

 i) **Ti** ho già invitato.

 j) Non **vi** vogliamo offendere.

3.10 Prepositions and the verbs essere and avere

3.10.1 Fill in the gaps choosing the correct option:

 a) Viaggio spesso 1. _____ lavoro perché 2. _____un agente 3. _____commercio. Mi vesto sempre elegante 4. _____la giacca.

1. a) **per**, b) di, c) sul

2. a) siete, b) sei, c) **sono**

3. a) per, b) **di**, c) nel

4. a) alla, b) **con**, c) della

b) Amo viaggiare perché posso prendermi una pausa 1. _____impegni d'ufficio. 2. _____Brasile ci vado ogni anno; mi piace camminare 3. _____strade piene 4. _____colori e gente.

1. a) sulle, b) **dagli**, c) degli

2. a) **in**, b) per, c) a

3. a) **per**, b) sulle, c) nella

4. a) nel, b) a, c) **di**

c) Mi sono trasferita 1. _____Italia 2. _____amore e ora 3. _____ a Roma 4. _____fare un corso di italiano

1. a) a, b) nell', c) **in**

2. a) all', b) di, c) **per**

3. a) siamo, b) è, c) **sono**

4. a) del, b) **per**, c) a

d) 1. _____due fratelli e una sorella; Maria invece 2. _____solo un fratello e 3. _____molto simili.

e) 1. a) **ho**, b) abbiamo, c) avete

f) 2. a) **ha**, b) hai, c) hanno

g) 3. a) siamo, b) **sono**, c) siete

h) Noi oggi 1. _____ delle cose da fare 2. _____centro; vieni 3. _____noi? C' 4. _____anche Giovanna.

1. a) ho, b) **abbiamo**, c) avete

2. a) al, b) per, c) **in**

3. a) di, b) nel, c) **con**

4. a) **è**, b) ha, c) sono

Answer keys

3.11 Demonstratives and possessive adjectives

3.11.1 Fill in the gaps with the correct demonstrative adjective:

a) **Questa** qui davanti è casa mia, **quella** in fondo alla strada è di mia sorella.

b) Non mi piace **questo/quel** dolce.

c) Chi è **quella** ragazza seduta laggiù?

d) Ragazzi, **questo** qui è il mio amico Gianni.

e) **Quello/questo** arco è l'arco di Costantino.

f) Metto le scarpe da ginnastica o **queste** qui con il tacco?

g) **Questo** è il mio libro di italiano, **quello** sul tavolo è il vostro.

h) **Questi** sono i miei genitori, Mario e Lucia.

i) **Questo/quello** è il volo per Milano.

j) In **questa** classe dove siamo noi c'è la lezione di storia, **quegli** studenti laggiù vanno alla lezione di filosofia.

3.11.2 Fill in the gaps with the correct possessive adjective or pronoun:

a) Piero ci ha invitati a cena a casa **sua**.

b) Mi piace la **tua** borsa; dove l'hai presa?

c) I **nostri** genitori sono andati al cinema con il **nostro** fratello più piccolo.

d) I **miei** amici mi aiutano sempre.

e) Ragazze, dove sono le **vostre** amiche?

f) La **nostra** cultura è molto interessante perché siamo un popolo antico.

g) Bambini, chi sono i **vostri** genitori?

h) La **nostra** fortuna è stata che vi abbiamo incontrati.

i) Mario e Susanna hanno cambiato macchina, la **loro** era molto vecchia.

j) Devo chiamare Giulia e dirle che la **sua** macchina è pronta.

3.12 Presente indicativo

<u>3.12.1 Fill in the gaps with the correct form of the 1st person singular of the presente indicativo of verbs in brackets:</u>

Ciao, 1. **mi chiamo** Thomas e 2. **sono** di Cracovia, ma 3. **abito** a Roma da qualche mese. Per adesso 4. **vivo** in albergo ma 5. **cerco** casa. Da un po' di tempo 6. **guardo** gli annunci online ma non 7. **trovo** nulla di interessante. Domani 8. **vado** in agenzia e 9. **spero** di trovare una persona che mi aiuti. 10. **ho** molta fiducia.

<u>3.12.2 Fill in the gaps with the correct form of the 3rd person singular of the presente indicativo of verbs in brackets:</u>

Lui 1. **si chiama** Thomas e 2. **è** di Cracovia, ma 3. **abita** a Roma da qualche mese. Per adesso 4. **vive** in albergo ma 5. **cerca** casa. Da un po' di tempo 6. **guarda** gli annunci online ma non 7. **trova** nulla di interessante. Domani 8. **va** in agenzia e 9. **spera** di trovare una persona che lo aiuti. 10. **ha** molta fiducia.

3.13 Past tenses

<u>3.13.1 Fill in the gaps with the correct form of the passato prossimo or imperfetto of verbs in brackets:</u>

Un pappagallo 1. **è scappato** di casa: 2. **è successo** qualche giorno fa a Milano. I proprietari 3. **erano** molto tristi ma 4. **hanno raccontato** la storia del pappagallo ai giornali. 5. **Si chiamava** Ugo e per loro 6. **era** come un figlio. Lo 7. **lasciavano** sempre libero in casa, ma un giorno il vento 8. **ha aperto** la finestra e lui 9. **è volato** via. Fortunatamente lo 10. **hanno ritrovato** pochi giorni dopo grazie all'aiuto di molti cittadini.

3.14 Combined personal pronouns

<u>3.14.1 Fill in the gaps with the correct combined personal pronoun:</u>

a) Porto alla nonna la torta - **Gliela** porto.

I am taking it to her.

b) Ci scrivi il tuo indirizzo? - **Ce lo** scrivi?

Can you write it to us?

c) Per Natale regalo un viaggio a Mario - **Glielo** regalo per Natale.

I am giving it to her for Christmas.

d) Chi vi presta la macchina per il viaggio? - Chi **ve la** presta?

Who is lending it to you?

e) Hanno scritto un messaggio ai loro amici - **Gliel'** hanno scritto.

They have written it to them.

f) Mi spieghi l'esercizio che non l'ho capito? - **Me lo** spieghi che non l'ho capito?

Could you explain it to me?

g) Avete chiesto a Paola se voleva venire anche lei? - **Glielo** avete chiesto?

Did you ask her about it?

h) Ti hanno già consegnato il pacco? - **Te lo** hanno già consegnato?

Have they already delivered it to you?

i) Avete comprato i cioccolatini al nonno? - **Glieli** avete comprati?

Have you bought them for him?

j) Ho regalato una collana alla mia fidanzata - **Gliel'**ho regalata.

I have given it to her

Section 4 – Dialogues

In this section, you will see the practical use of all the grammar seen in sections 1 and 2.

4.1 Basic greetings

"Ciao" is internationally known and used, but in many countries, it is used only to greet when it is time to go. In Italian, "ciao" represents the informal greeting, both when you meet a person and when you leave. Going away, you can also say, "ci vediamo" - see you. If you want to be formal when you meet a person, you may greet him or her using "salve", which is generic and can be used during any moment of the day. Of course, you can always say "buongiorno", if it is morning, and "buonasera" for the evening, which starts at sunset. Still being formal and wanting to greet someone when going away, you may use "arrivederci" or "buonanotte" after dinner. Please consider that "buongiorno" and "buonanotte" can also be used in informal contexts. Furthermore, there are the expressions "buona giornata" and "buona serata", which mean "have a good day" and "have a good evening/night".

4.2 The time

This is not a difficult topic if you consider that, in Italian, you tell the hour beforehand and the minutes right afterward. See the main translations: "o'clock" will be "in punto", but it is also possible to leave it out; "half" is "mezzo" and "quarter" is "un quarto". Now consider that when English uses "past" (to say minutes passed after the hour), Italian uses "e" (to add passed minutes to the hour); when English uses "to" (to say minutes left to the next hour), Italian uses "meno" (to indicate minutes that are left to the hour). English always uses "is", while Italian uses "sono"—hours are plural except "one", which uses "è" because it is the only one to be singular. Here are some examples:

It's four o'clock - sono le quattro (in punto)

It's quarter past four - sono le quattro e un quarto

It's half past four - sono le quattro e mezzo

It's quarter to five - sono le cinque meno un quarto

It's five to five - sono le cinque meno cinque

As you can see, in Italian, you tell the hour beforehand and the minutes that are passed or left right afterward.

Moreover, "midnight" corresponds to "mezzanotte" and "midday" to "mezzogiorno", and they are used with "è". For example: "è mezzanotte".

4.3 Introducing yourself

4.3.1 Informal - informale

a. Ciao! Io mi chiamo Maria, tu come ti chiami?

Hi! My name is Maria, what's your name?

b. Ciao! Mi chiamo Paul, molto piacere

Hi! My name is Paul, nice to meet you.

a. Piacere mio! Di dove sei?

Nice to meet you too! Where are you from?

b. Sono dell'Inghilterra ma vivo a Roma da tre anni. Studio medicina all'università. Tu?

I'm from England, but I've been living in Rome for three years. I study medicine at university. You?

a. Sono italiana, vengo da Napoli ma anch'io vivo a Roma e lavoro in una banca. Quanti anni hai? Io ne ho 26.

I'm Italian, I come from Naples, but I live in Rome just like you and work in a bank. How old are you? I'm 26.

b. Ho 23 anni ma tra poco ne compio 24.

I'm 23, but I'm turning 24 soon.

4.3.2. Formal – formale

a. Buongiono, Signora, come posso aiutarla?

Good morning, Madame, how can I help you?

b. Buongiorno, dovrei iscrivermi al corso di yoga.

Good morning, I would like to join the yoga class.

a. Bene, come si chiama?

Good, what's your name?

b. Mi chiamo Sonia.

My name is Sonia.

a. Qual è il suo cognome?

What's your last name?

b. Rossi.

a. Quando è nata? (data di nascita)

When were you born? (date of birth)

b. Sono nata il 4 agosto del 1983 a Milano.

I was born on August 4th, 1983, in Milan.

a. Dove vive?

Where do you live?

b. Vivo qui a Milano.

I live here in Milan.

a. Qual è il suo indirizzo?

What's your address?

b. Via Bragazzi 20

a. Che lavoro fa?

What's your job?

b. Sono un'insegnante.

I'm a teacher.

a. Mi lascia il suo numero di cellulare e un indirizzo email?

Could you give me your phone number and email address?

b. Certamente! Il mio numero di cellulare è 36298465 e il mio indirizzo email è s.rossi@xmail.com (esse punto rossi chiocciola xmail punto com)

Sure! My phone number is 36298465 and my email address is s.rossi@xmail.com (es dot rossi at xmail dot com)

a. Perfetto, ora firmi qui per cortesia.

Perfect, now sign here, please.

b. Ecco.

Here you are.

a. Arrivederci signora Rossi.

Bye-bye.

b. Arrivederci.

Bye-bye.

4.3.3 Questions

1. Di dov'è Paul?

Where is Paul from?

2. Di dov'è Maria?

Where is Maria from?

3. Che cosa studia Paul?

What does Paul study?

    4. Dove vivono Paul e Maria?

Where do Paul and Maria live?

    5. Che lavoro fa Maria?

What is Maria's job?

    6. Quanti anni ha Paul?

How old is Paul?

    7. Quando è nata la signora Sonia?

When was Mrs. Sonia born?

    8. Che lavoro fa la signora Sonia?

What is Mrs. Sonia's job?

    9. Come si chiama la signora Sonia di cognome?

What is Mrs. Sonia's surname?

    10. Dove vive la signora Sonia?

Where does Mrs. Sonia live?

4.3.4 Answer keys

    1. Dell'Inghilterra.

From England.

    2. Di Napoli.

From Naples.

    3. Medicina.

Medicine.

    4. A Roma.

In Rome.

    5. Lavora in banca.

She works in a bank.

    6. 23.

7. Il 4 agosto del 1983.

On August 4th, 1983.

8. L'insegnante.

The teacher.

9. Rossi

10. A Milano.

In Milan.

4.3.5 Informal - informale: meeting people in a club - conoscere persone in un locale

a. Nicola; b. Alessandro; c. Martina; d. Laura; e. Barman - barista

b. Che bel locale, non c'ero mai stato prima, è nuovo?

What a nice club? I have never been here before, is it new?

a. Sì, lo hanno aperto circa due mesi fa. Ci sono venuto per la prima volta la settimana scorsa con mio fratello e alcuni suoi amici. Ci siamo divertiti molto.

Yes, it is. It opened about two months ago. I first came here last week with my brother and some friends of his. We had a lot of fun.

b. Prendiamo qualcosa da bere?

Shall we get a drink?

a. Certo!

Sure!

e. Buonasera, ragazzi, che cosa vi preparo?

Goodnight, guys, what can I prepare for you?

a. Per me un vodka - tonic

For me a vodka-tonic

b. Anche per me grazie.

I'll go with the same one, thanks.

e. Ecco qui, sono 14 euro.

Here you are, it is 14 euros.

b. Lascia, offro io!

No, I got it!

a. Grazie, il prossimo giro è mio!

Thank you, next round is on me!

b. Guarda quelle due ragazze laggiù, quelle vicino alla porta; non sono carine?

Look at those girls over there, the ones near the door; aren't they nice?

a. Ah, Alessandro si è messo subito al lavoro! Andiamo a conoscerle!

Ah, Alessandro immediately begun to work! Let's go and meet them!

b. Naturalmente, mi sono lasciato ormai da un mese ed è ora di conoscere nuove ragazze!

Of course, I broke up almost one month ago and it is time to meet new girls!

a. Ciao, ragazze, possiamo sederci con voi al vostro tavolo?

Hi, girls, can we take a seat with you at your table?

d. Va bene; c'è abbastanza spazio per tutti.

That's ok; there is enough space for everyone.

b. Piacere, mi chiamo Alessandro e lui è Nicola. Voi?

My name is Alessandro, nice to meet you. He is Nicola, and you?

d. Io mi chiamo Laura e questa è mia cugina, Martina.

My name is Laura and this is my cousin, Martina.

a. Venite spesso qui?

Do you often come here?

c. Da quando ha aperto siamo venute 2 volte; è un bel locale, e la musica è molto bella.

Since it has opened, we came here twice; it is a nice club, and the music is very good.

b. Hai ragione; è la prima volta che vengo ma ci tornerò sicuramente. Possiamo offrirvi qualcosa da bere?

You're right; this is the first time I come here, but I will definitely come back. Can we offer you something to drink?

c. Per me, no, grazie. Non bevo.

For me, no, thanks. I don't drink.

d. Per me, si, grazie.

For me, yes, please.

b. Che cosa ti posso prendere?

What can I get for you?

d. Un vodka-tonic.

A vodka-tonic.

b. Lo stesso che stiamo bevendo noi! Abbiamo già una cosa in comune...

The same drink we are having! We've already something in common...

[Alessando e Laura vanno a prendere da bere e tornano]

[Alessando and Laura go to order the drink and come back]

a. Martina mi stava raccontando che avere un negozio di vestiti in centro.

Martina was telling me you have a clothing shop downtown.

d. Sì, lo abbiamo aperto tre anni fa. Voi cosa fate, ragazzi?

Yes, we opened it three years ago. What do you do, guys?

a. Io sono avvocato, lavoro in uno studio legale che si occupa di cause civili.

I am an attorney; I work in a law firm, which deals with civil cases.

b. Io sono architetto, e lavoro come libero professionista e ho il mio ufficio a casa.

I am an architect, and I work freelance and have got my own office at home.

a. Basta con le domande; andiamo a ballare!

Enough with questions; let's go dancing!

b.c. e d. Andiamo!

Let's go!

4.3.5.1 Questions

1. Alessandro e Nicola sono mai stati in questo locale?

Have Alessandro and Nicola ever been to this club?

2. Che cosa prenodono da bere?

What do they drink?

3. Chi paga?

Who pays?

4. Che cosa chiede Nicola alle ragazze per conoscerle?

What does Nicola ask the girls (in order) to get to know them?

5. È la prima volta che Martina e Laura vanno in questo locale?

Is it the first time Martina and Laura go to this club?

6. Che cosa prendono Martina e Laura da bere?

What do Martina and Laura get to drink?

7. Con chi va Laura a prendere da bere?

Who does Laura go to get a drink with?

8. Cosa stava raccontando Martina a Nicola mentre gli altri erano a prendere da bere?

What was Martina telling Nicola while the others were getting drinks?

9. Che lavoro fanno Alessandro e Nicola, lavorano insieme?

What is Alessandro and Nicola's job? Do they work together?

10. Dove vanno insieme dopo essersi conosciuti?

Where do they go together after they had met?

4.3.5.2 Answer keys

1. Per Alessandro è la prima volta; Nicola invece c'è stato la settimana prima con suo fratello e alcuni suoi amici.

For Alessandro, it is the first time; while Nicola has been there the previous week with his brother and some friends of his.

2. Prendono due vodka-tonic.

They get two vodka-tonic.

3. Paga Alessandro; Nicola pagherà il giro dopo.

Alessandro pays; Nicola will pay the next round.

4. Gli chiede se possono sedersi con loro al loro tavolo.

He asks them if they can take a seat with them at their table.

5. No, è la seconda volta che ci vanno da quando ha aperto.

No, it is not. It is the second time they go there since it opened.

6. Laura prende un vodka-tonic; Martina niente perché non beve.

Laura gets a vodka-tonic; Martina nothing because she does not drink.

7. Con Alessandro.

With Alessandro.

8. Martina gli stava raccontando che Laura e lei hanno un negozio di vestiti in centro.

Martina was telling him that she and Laura have a clothing shop downtown.

9. Alessandro è un architetto e Nicola un avvocato. Non lavorano insieme perché Nicola lavora in uno studio legale e Alessandro è un libero professionista e ha il suo ufficio a casa.

Alessandro is an architect and Nicola is an attorney. They do not work together because Nicola works in a law office, and Alessandro is a freelancer and has got his own office at home.

10. Dopo essersi conosciuti vanno a ballare.

After they had met, they go dancing.

4.4 Buying and ordering

4.4.1 In a shop - in un negozio

a. Shop assistant - commesso; b. client - cliente

a. Buongiorno, posso aiutarla?

Good morning, can I help you?

b. Buongiorno, si. Vorrei provarmi quei pantaloni blu che sono in vetrina.

Good morning, yes. I would like to try on those blue trousers in the shop window.

a. Certo, che taglia le serve?

Sure, what size do you need?

b. Una small.

A small.

[il cliente entra nel camerino]

[the client goes into the fitting room]

a. Come le vanno?

How do they suit you?

b. Mi sembra bene, però vorrei provare anche la taglia più grande.

I think well, but I would like to try on also the bigger size.

a. Gliela prendo subito.

I'll take it immediately.

[il cliente entra nel camerino]

[the client goes into the fitting room]

b. Questi mi vanno decisamente meglio; è la mia taglia.

These suit me much better; it's my size.

a. Vuole vedere una camicia da abbinare al pantalone?

Would you like to see a shirt to match with the trousers?

b. No grazie, va bene così. Quanto costano?

No thanks, it's ok. How much do they cost?

a. Costano 120 euro. Paga in contanti, bancomat, o carta di credito?

They cost 120 euros. Do you pay by cash, debit, or credit card?

b. Carta di credito.

Credit card.

a. Posso avere un documento d'identità, per favore?

Could you give me an ID, please?

b. Certo, eccolo.

Sure, here you are.

a. Perfetto. Questo è il suo scontrino e questo il suo sacchetto. Arrivederci.

Perfect. Here is your receipt and your bag. Bye-bye.

b. Arrivederci.

Bye-bye.

4.4.1.1 Questions

1. Che cosa vuole provare il cliente?

What does the client want to try on?

2. Che taglia compra alla fine?

What size does he finally buy?

3. Che cosa la commessa gli propone da abbinare?

What does the shop assistant propose to match them with?

4. Quanto costano i pantaloni?

How much do the trousers cost?

5. Come paga il cliente?

How does the client pay?

4.4.1.2 Answer keys

1. Un paio di pantaloni blu.

A pair of blue trousers.

2. Una medium.

A medium.

3. Una camicia.

A shirt.

4. 120 euro.

120 euros.

5. Con carta di credito.

With credit card.

4.4.2. Buying online - comprare online

a. Ciao, Elena, come stai?

Hi, Elena, how are you?

b. Ciao, Sonia! Bene, grazie. Tu?

Hi, Sonia! Fine, thanks. You?

a. Bene. Hai visto i saldi sul sito magia.com?

I'm good. Have you seen the sales on the website magia.com?

b. Non ancora. Hai fatto buoni affari?

Not yet. Have you made good deals?

a. Sì. Ho comprato un paio di scarpe con il tacco e una borsa di pelle nera al 50% di sconto. Nel carrello ho anche un paio di jeans ma c'è stato un problema con il pagamento, non mi fa procedere all'acquisto. È molto strano perché compro spesso su questo sito e il mio account non ha mai avuto problemi.

Yes. I bought a pair of heels and a black leather bag purse with 50% discount. In the cart, I also have a pair of jeans, but there's a problem with the paying process – I can't proceed with the purchase. It's very strange, as I often buy items on this website and my account has never had problems.

b. Hai provato a ricaricare la pagina?

Have you tried to refresh the page?

a. Si, ma non è successo nulla. Stasera riprovo e se non funziona contatterò il servizio clienti. Non voglio perdere quei jeans e non voglio pagare due spedizioni.

Yes, but nothing happened. Tonight, I'm trying again, and if it doesn't work, I'll contact the customer service.

b. Non ti preoccupare, vedrai che stasera ci riesci. Una volta è capitato anche a me. Volevo prenotare un volo Roma-Parigi ma il sito non caricava la pagina del pagamento. Ci ho provato il giorno dopo e ha funzionato.

Don't worry. You'll see – you'll sort it out tonight. Once it happened to me too. I wanted to book a Rome-Paris flight, but the website didn't load the payment page.

a. Bene, ti farò sapere come è andata a finire.

Good, I'll let you know how it goes.

4.4.2.1 Questions

1. Dove ha fatto acquisti Sonia?

Where has Sonia shopped?

2. Che cosa ha comprato?

What has she bought?

3. Che problema ha avuto Sonia con i Jeans?

What problem did she have with jeans?

4. Che cosa le suggerisce di fare Elena?

What does Elena suggest she do?

5. Quando Elena ha avuto un problema simile a quello di Sonia?

Did Elena have a similar problem to Sonia's one and when?

4.4.2.2 Answer keys

1. Su magia.com

On magia.com.

2. Un paio di pantaloni e una borsa di pelle.

A pair of trousers and a leather bag.

3. Il sito non le caricava la pagina per il pagamento.

The website didn't upload the payment page.

4. Di ricaricare la pagina.

To refresh the page.

5. Quando voleva prenotare un volo Roma-Parigi.

When she wanted to book a Rome-Paris flight.

4.5 At work

4.5.1 Getting ready for a meeting – preparandosi per una riunione.

a. Buongiorno, Giulia!

Good morning, Giulia!

b. Buongiorno, Signor Carli!

Good morning, Mr. Carli!

a. Oggi abbiamo molto lavoro da fare e sono arrivato in ritardo perché c'era molto traffico.

Today, we have a lot of work to do and I arrived late because there was a lot of traffic.

b. Lo so; ho già stampato tutta la documentazione per la riunione di oggi, anche l'ordine del giorno.

I know; I've already printed all documentation of the meeting today, the agenda too.

a. Brava, ottimo lavoro! A che ora arriva il consiglio?

Good, good job! What time does the board arrive?

b. Tra un'ora, alle 10.

In one hour, at 10 o'clock.

a. Bene, abbiamo ancora tempo. Allora, apri la cartella "fatture" sul mio computer e stampa tutte quelle dell'ultimo mese. Poi controlla la tua email e scarica tutti i file che ti ho inviato ieri sera e stampali.

Well, we still have time. So, open the folder "invoices" on my laptop and download all of the last month. Then check your email and download all files I sent you yesterday and print them.

b. Va bene, lo faccio subito. Ecco qui!

Ok, I'll do it right now. Here you are!

a. Queste sono le indicazioni per il mese, per i venditori e la dirigenza. Dove sono i curricula da analizzare per i posti vacanti?

These are indications for the month, for the salespeople and the management. Where are the CVs that have to be analyzed for open positions?

b. Li ha la responsabile delle risorse umane; sono già selezionati per i colloqui.

The HR has them; they are already selected for interviews.

a. Ho preparato il piano per gli incentivi e compensi per il prossimo semestre e anche per gli stipendi. Ho qualche appuntamento dopo?

I've also prepared the planning for bonuses and commissions for next semester and also for wages. Do I have any appointments after?

b. No, le ho cancellato tutti gli appuntamenti della giornata. Dovrebbe solo fare una chiamata al Signor Bassi per chiudere l'accordo della settimana scorsa.

No, you haven't. I've cleared your schedule for the day. You may only make a call to Mr. Bassi to close last week's agreement.

a. Molto bene, allora direi che abbiamo tutto pronto. Sei un'ottima segretaria.

Very well, so I'd say we have everything ready. You're a perfect secretary.

b. La ringrazio Signor Carli, lei è un capo eccezionale.

Thank you, Mr. Carli, you're an excellent boss.

4.5.2 Questions

1. Perché il Signor Carli è arrivato tardi al lavoro?

Why did Mr. Carli arrive late at work?

2. Che cosa ha già stampato Giulia?

What has Giulia already printed?

3. A che ora arriva il consiglio?

What time does the board arrive?

4. Dove sono i file che Giulia deve stampare dal computer?

Where are the files Giulia has to print from the computer?

5. Che altro deve stampare Giulia?

What else does Giulia have to print?

6. Che cosa ha preparato il Signor Carli per i venditori e la dirigenza?

What did Mr. Carli prepare for salespersons and the management?

7. Chi ha i curricula per le posizioni aperte?

Who has the CVs for the open positions?

8. Che cosa ha già preparato il Signor Carli per il semestre successivo?

What has Mr. Carli already prepared for the following semester?

9. Quali altri impegni ha il Signor Carli per la giornata?

What other appointments does Mr. Carli have for the day?

10. Perché Giulia ringrazia il Signor Carli?

Why did Giulia thank Mr. Carli?

4.5.3 Answer keys

1. Perché c'era molto traffico.

Because there was a lot of traffic.

2. La documentazione per il meeting e l'ordine del giorno.

The documentation for the meeting and the agenda.

3. Alle dieci.

At ten o'clock.

4. Nella cartella "fatture".

In the "invoices" folder.

5. I file che il Signor Carli le ha mandato la sera prima via email.

Files Mr. Carli sent her the night before.

6. Le indicazioni del mese.

Instructions for the month.

7. La responsabile delle risorse umane.

The HR head.

8. Gli incentivi, i compensi, e gli stipendi.

Bonuses, commissions, and wages.

9. Deve solo chiamare il Signor Bassi per chiudere l'accordo della settimana prima.

He only has to call Mr. Bassi to close the agreement of the week before.

10. Perché le ha detto che è un'ottima segretaria.

Because he told her she is a great secretary.

4.6 At school

4.6.1 First day at the college – primo giorno all'università

a./b. students; c. professor

a. Scusami, sai dov'è la lezione del Professor Fossa? È il mio primo giorno all'università e devo ancora orientarmi. Ci sono molte aule e non so ancora dove sono.

Excuse me, do you know where Professor Fossa's lesson is? It's my first day at college, and I still have to find my bearings. There are many classrooms, and I don't know where they are yet.

b. Certo! Capisco, i primi giorni sono sempre i più difficili, ma vedrai che in meno di una settimana saprai orientarti alla perfezione. Comunque, io sto andando proprio alla sua lezione, quindi seguimi.

Sure! I know, first days are always the most difficult, but you will see – in less than one week, you will be able to orient yourself perfectly. Anyway, I'm going exactly to his class, so follow me.

a. Perfetto, sono stato proprio fortunato. Comunque io mi chiamo Pietro.

Perfect, I've been very lucky. I'm Pietro by the way.

b. Piacere. Io mi chiamo Luca. Di dove sei?

Nice to meet you. I'm Luca. Where are you from?

a. Sono di Rimini e tu?

I'm from Rimini, and you?

b. Anch'io! Come è possibile che non ci siamo mai visti prima? Rimini è una città piccola.

Me too! How is it possible that you have never met before? Rimini is a small town.

a. In effetti è incredibile. Quanti anni hai?

It is indeed unbelievable. How old are you?

b. Ho 20 anni. Tu?

I'm 20, you?

a. Io ho 19 anni. Quindi abbiamo più o meno la stessa età. Che scuola hai frequentato?

I'm 19. So, we are the same age, more or less. Which school did you attend?

b. Mi sono diplomato all'istituto tecnico, tu?

I graduated at the technical institute, you?

a. Anch'io, ma a quello di Cattolica, perché prima vivevo lì con la mia famiglia. Ci siamo trasferiti quando ero al secondo anno e non volevo cambiare scuola.

Me too, but in Cattolica, because I used to live there with my family. We moved when I was in my second year, and I didn't want to change school.

b. Facevi un lungo viaggio tutte le mattine!

You took a long drive every morning!

a. Si, infatti mi svegliavo molto presto. In autobus ci voleva un'ora, ma quando mi portava mio padre in macchina potevo alzarmi un pochino dopo.

Yes, I did. I used to wake up early. It took one hour by bus, but when my father took me by car, I could wake up a bit later.

b. Ok, siamo arrivati! Questa è l'aula del Professor Fossa. È molto bravo ma anche molto esigente, infatti lo scorso anno non ho passato l'esame e ora deve rifrequentare le lezioni.

Ok, we've arrived! This is Professor Fossa's classroom. He is very good but very demanding too, in fact I didn't pass the exam last year and now I have to attend his lessons again.

c. Buongiorno, a tutti! Sono il Professor Fossa and e questo è il corso di Meccatronica. Alcuni di voi sono nuovi studenti, quindi benvenuti. Altri sono vecchi studenti e quindi, ben tornati. Come i vostri compagni, quelli che non hanno passato l'esame lo scorso anno, posso dirvi che sono molto esigente, ma se frequentate le lezioni e prendete appunti sono sicuro che passerete l'esame senza alcun problema. Per qualsiasi domanda, vi prego di venirmi a trovare nel mio ufficio. Sarò lieto di rispondere ai vostri quesiti. Il mio orario di ricevimento è lunedì e venerdì dalle 9 del mattino alle 13; mercoledì e giovedì dalle 2 alle 5 del pomeriggio. Se avete qualche problema a venire in questi giorni e orari, per favore scrivetemi una email e prenderemo un appuntamento.

Good morning, everyone! I'm Professor Fossa, and this is the Mechatronics course. Some of you are new students, so welcome. Others are old students, and so, welcome back. As your classmates, those who didn't pass the exam last year, can tell you, I'm very demanding, but if you attend classes and take note, I'm sure you will pass the exam without any kind of problems. For any questions, please come to visit me in my office. I'll be glad to answer your queries. My office hours are Monday and Friday from 9 am to 1 pm; Wednesday and Thursday from 2 pm to 5 pm. If you have any difficulties to come on these days and times, please write me an email, and we will set up an appointment.

a. Non sembra così cattivo come dici!

He doesn't seem to be as bad as you said!

b. Fidati, lo vedrai all'esame!

Trust me, you will see at the exam!

c. Ok, per oggi è tutto. Ci vediamo la prossima settimana.

Ok, that's all for today. See you next week.

b. Vado in biblioteca per mettere in ordine gli appunti, vieni con me?

I'm going to the library to order notes, are you coming with me?

a. Si, perché no! Così imparo anche dove si trova.

Yes, why not! So I also learn where it is.

b. Perfetto! Ti mostro anche la mensa; è di strada.

Perfect! I'll show you the canteen too; it's on the way.

4.6.2 Questions

1. Quale aula sta cercando Pietro?

What classroom is Pietro looking for?

2. Da dove viene Luca?

Where is Luca from?

3. Quale scuola ha frequentato? E Pietro?

Which school did he attend? And Pietro?

4. Perchè Pietro ha frequentato la scuola a Cattolica?

Why did Pietro attend the school in Cattolica?

5. Come andava a scuola Pietro?

How did Pietro used to go to school?

6. Perché Luca frequenta di nuovo le lezioni del Professor Fossa?

Why is Luca attending Professor Fossa's classes again?

7. Quali sono i consigli del Professor Fossa per passare l'esame?

What are Professor Fossa's tips to pass the exam?

8. Quali sono i giorni di ricevimento del Professor Fossa?

What is Professor Fossa's office time?

9. Dove vanno Pietro e Luca dopo la lezione?

Where are Pietro and Luca going after the class?

10. Che cosa Luca mostrerà a Pietro?

What is Luca going to show Pietro?

4.6.3 Answer keys

1. Pietro sta cercando l'aula del Professor Fossa.

Pietro is looking for Professor Fossa's classroom.

2. Luca viene da Rimini.

Luca comes from Rimini.

3. Tutti e due hanno frequentato l'istituto tecnico.

They both attended the technical institute.

4. Perché viveva lì con la sua famiglia e quando si sono trasferiti Pietro non voleva cambiare scuola.

Because they lived there with his family and when they moved, Pietro didn't want to change school.

5. In autobus o in macchina con suo padre.

By bus or by car with his father.

6. Perché non ha passato l'esame l'anno precedente.

Because he didn't pass the exam the previous year.

7. Frequentare le lezioni e prendere appunti.

To attend classes and take notes.

8. Lunedì, mercoledì, giovedì, e venerdì.

Monday, Wednesday, Thursday, and Friday.

9. In biblioteca.

At the library.

10. La mensa.

The canteen.

4.7 Traveling

4.7.1 At the station – alla stazione

a. traveler b. station worker

a. Buonasera, vorrei un'informazione.

Good evening, I would like information.

b. Buonasera a lei, mi dica pure.

Good evening to you, please tell me.

a. Vorrei sapere quando parte il prossimo treno per Roma; ho finito di lavorare tardi, e ho perso quello delle 16:40.

I would like to know when the next train to Rome is leaving; I finished work late, and I missed the 16:40 one.

b. Ce n'è uno alle 17:00 e un altro alle 17:30. Quello delle 17:00 arriva alle 18:30 perché è un treno regionale e fa alcune fermate intermedie, e costa 15 euro. Quello delle 17:30 invece è un diretto; anche quello arriva alle 18 e costa 28 euro.

There is one at 17:00 and another at 17:30. The one at 17:00 arrives at 18:30 because it is a regional train and has some extra stops, it costs 15 euros. The one at 17:30 is direct; it also arrives at 18:30 and costs 28 euros.

a. Allora prenderò quello delle 17:00, così non aspetto troppo tempo in stazione. Dove posso comprare i biglietti?

So, I will take the 17:00 one, so I'm not waiting too much in the station. Where can I buy tickets?

b. In biglietteria, ma se c'è coda le conviene andare alla biglietteria automatica.

At the ticket office, if there is a line, it is better for you to go to the ticket machine.

a. E posso pagare con carta di credito anche alla biglietteria automatica?

And can I pay by credit card at the ticket machine too?

b. Certamente. Accetta contanti, bancomat, e carta di credito.

Sure. It accepts cash, debit, and credit cards.

a. Va bene, grazie. Un'ultima cosa: da quale binario parte il treno?

Ok, thanks. One last thing: Which platform does the train leave from?

b. Dal binario 8. Per fare prima usi il sottopassaggio.

From platform 8. To be faster, use the underpass.

a. Perfetto, grazie.

Perfect, thank you.

4.7.1.1 Questions

1. Che treno ha perso il viaggiatore?

What train does the traveler lose?

2. Perché ha perso il treno?

Why did he lose the train?

3. Quali treni può prendere dopo?

Which trains can he take after?

4. Quale treno arriva prima? Perché?

Which train does arrive before? Why?

5. Quale treno costa meno?

Which train does cost less?

6.Quale decide di prendere il viaggiatore? Perché?

Which does the traveler decide to take? Why?

7.Dove può comprare i biglietti?

Where can he buy tickets?

8.Può pagare in contanti alla biglietteria automatica?

Can he pay by cash at the ticket machine?

9.Da che binario parte il treno?

Which platform does the train leave from?

10.Come può raggiungere quel binario?

How can he reach the platform?

4.7.1.2 Answer keys

1. Quello delle 16:40.

The 16:40 one.

2. Perché ha finito di lavorare tardi.

Because he finished work late.

3. Può prendere quello delle 17:00 e quello delle 17:30

He can take the 17:00 and 17:30 ones.

4. Arrivano tutti e due alle 18:30 perché quello delle 17:30 è un treno diretto e non ha fermate intermedie, mentre quello delle 17:00 è un treno regionale e ha fermate intermedie.

They both arrive at 18:30 because the 17:30 is a direct train and doesn't do extra stops, while the 17:00 is a regional train and has extra stops.

5. Quello regionale.

The regional one.

6. Quello regionale così non deve aspettare troppo in stazione.

The regional one so he does not have to wait too much in the station.

7. Sia in biglietteria che alla biglietteria automatica.

Both at the ticket office and at the ticket machine.

8. No, può pagare anche con bancomat o carta di credito.

No, he can also pay with debit or credit cards.

9. Dal binario 8.

From platform 8.

10. Con il sottopassaggio.

By the underpass.

4.7.2 At the airport – all'aeroporto

a./b. travelers; c. airline company employee

a. Bene, siamo arrivati. Ora, questo è il terminal degli arrivi e noi dobbiamo andare a quello delle partenze dei voli internazionali che è là.

Well, we've arrived. Further up is the arrivals terminal and we have to go to the international departures terminal that is there.

b. Ok, allora scarichiamo le valigie.

Ok, so let's unload our suitcases.

[al check-in]

[at the check-in]

c. Buongiorno! Prego, biglietti, passaporto, e mettete le valigie sulla bilancia.

Good morning, tickets, passports, and put your suitcases on the scale, please.

a. Ecco qui, Giulia, dammi il tuo.

Here you are. Giulia, give yours.

c. Avete solo queste due? Bagagli a mano?

Do you have only these two? Any hand luggage?

a. Sì, solo queste. Come bagaglio a mano abbiamo solo questo zaino.

Yes, only these ones. As hand luggage, we have only this backpack.

c. Bene, ci metta questa etichetta. Allora, queste sono le vostre carte d'imbarco, l'orario di apertura del gate è alle 10:20. Chiude alle 10:50. Ricordate che non sono ammessi liquidi sopra i 100 ml e ricordatevi di presentare la carta d'imbarco all'addetto alla sicurezza prima dei controlli. Ricordate inoltre di guardare i monitor circa 10 minuti prima dell'inizio dell'imbarco per conoscere il numero del gate.

Fine, so put this tag on. So, these are your boarding cards, gate opens at 10:20 and closes at 10:50. Remember that liquids over 100 ml are not allowed and remember to show the boarding card to the safety officer before the security control area. Remember also to look at screens about 10 minutes before boarding to check the gate number.

a. Tutto chiaro, grazie.

All clear, thanks.

b. Bene, abbiamo ancora un po' di tempo, così possiamo fare un giro per i negozi e mangiare qualcosa prima di imbarcarci.

Well, we still have some time, so we can take a walk around the shops and have something to eat before boarding.

a. Non siamo ancora partite e già vuoi comprare qualcosa? Per il ritorno dovremmo comprare una nuova valigia!

We haven't left yet and you already want to buy something? For the return, we should buy a new suitcase!

b. Hai ragione; aspetterò il ritorno per fare acquisti in aeroporto. Prendiamoci un caffè!

You're right; I will wait for the return to shop in the airport. Let's have a coffee!

a. Bell'idea e sicuramente più economica!

Good idea and definitely cheaper!

4.7.2.1 Questions

1. A quale terminal devono recarsi i viaggiatori?

Which terminal should the travelers go to?

2. Quanti bagagli hanno i viaggiatori?

How many suitcases do the travelers have?

3. Quanti bagagli a mano hanno i viaggiatori?

How many hand luggage do the travelers have?

4. Che cosa dà l'impiegato della compagnia aerea ai viaggiatori da mettere sul bagaglio a mano?

What does the airline employee give to the travelers to put on the hand luggage?

5. A che ora inizia l'imbarco? A che ora chiude il gate?

What time does the boarding start? What time does the gate close?

6. Che cosa devono mostrare i viaggiatori all'addetto alla sicurezza?

What do the travelers have to show to the safety officer?

7. Che cosa devono controllare i viaggiatori sul monitor 10 minuti prima dell'apertura del gate?

What do the travelers have to check on screens 10 minutes before the gate opens?

8. Che cosa vuole fare Giulia prima di imbarcarsi?

What does Giulia want to do before boarding?

9. Quando comprerà qualcosa in aeroporto?

When will she buy something in the airport?

10. Perché alla fine Giulia propone di prendere un caffè?

Why does Giulia propose to have a coffee?

4.7.2.2 Answer keys

1. Al terminal delle partenze internazionali.

At the international departure terminal.

2. Ne hanno due.

They have two.

3. Ne hanno uno.

They have one.

4. Un'etichetta.

A tag.

5. L'imbarco inizia alle 10:20 e chiude alle 10:50.

Boarding starts at 10:20 and closes at 10:50.

6. Il loro passaporto.

Their passports.

7. Il numero del gate.

The gate number.

8. Vuole comprare qualcosa.

She wants to buy something.

9. Perché la sua amica le dice che altrimenti dovrebbero comprare una valigia più grande per il ritorno.

Because her friend tells her they should buy another bigger suitcase for the return.

10. Al ritorno.

On the return.

4.7.3 Booking a hotel - prenotare un albergo

a. customer; b. receptionist

b. Albergo Serena buongiorno, sono Sara. Come posso aiutarla?

Hotel Serena good morning, Sara speaking. How can I help you?

a. Buongiorno, vorrei prenotare una stanza per la settimana dal 15 al 22 luglio.

Good morning, I would like to book a room for the week from 15th to 22nd July.

b. Una camera singola o doppia?

A single or a double room?

a. Una camera doppia, per cortesia.

A double room, please.

b. Mi faccia controllare. Per quella settimana abbiamo disponibile solo una camera vista mare.

Let me check. For that week, we have only a sea view room available.

a. E quanto costa?

And how much does it cost?

b. 90 euro al giorno con sola colazione inclusa.

90 euro per day with breakfast included.

a. C'è anche possibilità di scegliere la pensione completa?

Is there the opportunity to have full-board?

b. No, mi dispiace signora, al massimo potete scegliere la mezza pensione. Il nostro ristorante è aperto anche per cena, ma è solo alla carta.

No, there isn't, sorry. At most, you can have half-board. Our restaurant is open for dinner too but only a la carte.

a. Va bene, allora prenoterò la soluzione a mezza pensione. Quanto costa in più?

Ok, I will book the half-board solution. How much does it cost?

b. 20 euro al giorno. Consideri che deve anche aggiungere la tassa di soggiorno che è di 5 euro al giorno per persona.

20 euro per day. Consider that you have to add the local tax, which is 5 euro per day per person.

a. Va bene, voglio prenotare.

That's fine. I want to book.

b. Mi può fornire i suoi dati per cortesia?

Could you give me your personal information?

a. Certamente. Mi chiamo Manuela Fierro, nata il 03 marzo del 1976 a Bologna. Vivo a Bologna in via della Canonica numero 20.

Of course. My name is Manuela Fierro, born on March 3rd in 1976, in Bologna. I live in Bologna, via della Canonica number 20.

b. Un recapito telefonico e un indirizzo email, per favore?

A contact number and email, please?

a. Il mio numero di cellulare è 3749921564 e il mio indirizzo email è m.fierro@xmail.com

My cell phone number is 3749921564 and my email address is m.fierro@xmail.com.

b. Perfetto. Ora le invio una email con i dati per il pagamento con carta di credito o bonifico.

Perfect. I'm sending an email now with payment instructions by credit card or bank transfer.

a. Devo pagare tutto l'importo?

Do I have to pay the sum total?

b. No, solo la caparra. Salderà qui da noi il giorno della partenza. Ha tempo fino a 3 giorni prima per cancellare la prenotazione e, in quel caso, il deposito le verrà rimborsato completamente.

No, you don't. Only a down payment. You will pay the balance here on the departure day. You have until 3 days before to cancel your booking and, in this case, the down payment will be fully refunded.

a. Va bene. Mi può dare un'ulteriore informazione?

Ok. Could you give me further information?

b. Certamente, mi dica.

Sure, please tell me.

a. Affittate auto all'hotel?

Do you rent cars at the hotel?

b. No, ma non le consiglio di affittare un'auto. Non ci sono molti parcheggi, e i pochi che ci sono costano molto. Qui accanto c'è un negozio che affitta biciclette o motorini che sono più comodi per visitare le spiagge e raggiungere i punti d'interesse turistico della zona.

No, we don't. But I do not suggest you to rent a car. There are not many parking areas, and those few cost a lot. Here, next to the hotel, there is a shop that rents bicycles and motor scooters, which are more comfortable to reach beaches and local touristic points of interest.

a. Perfetto, molto gentile. Grazie mille.

Perfect, very kind. Thank you so much.

b. Non c'è di che, e l'aspettiamo. Arrivederci.

You are welcome, and we are waiting for you. Bye-bye.

a. Arrivederci.

Bye-bye.

4.7.3.1 Questions

1. Perché la cliente chiama l'albergo Serena?

Why is the client calling Hotel Serena?

2. Che camera ha disponibile l'albergo per la settimana dal 15 al 22 luglio?

Which room does the hotel have available for the week from 15th to 22nd July?

3. Quando costa con colazione inclusa?

How much does it cost with breakfast included?

4. L'albergo offre l'opzione pensione completa?

Does the hotel offer the full-board option?

5. Quanto costa la tassa di soggiorno?

How much does the local tax cost?

6. Dove è nata la signora Fierro?

Where was Mrs. Fierro Born?

7. Come potrà pagare l'albergo?

How will she be able to pay the hotel?

8. Se cancella due giorni prima, l'albergo le rimborsa il deposito?

If she cancels two days before, will the hotel refund her the down payment?

9. Che cosa chiede infine la signora Fierro alla receptionist?

What does Mrs. Fierro ask the receptionist?

10. Che cosa consiglia di affittare la receptionist al posto della macchina? Perché?

What does the receptionist suggest to rent instead of the car? Why?

4.7.3.2 Answer keys

1. Perché vuole prenotare una camera doppia per una settimana a luglio.

Because she wants to book a double room for one week in July.

2. Una camera vista mare.

A sea view room.

3. 90 euro al giorno.

90 euros per day.

4. No, perché il ristorante offre la cena solo alla carta.

No, it doesn't. Because the restaurant offers only dinner a la carte.

5. 5 euro al giorno per persona.

5 euro per day per person.

6. A Bologna.

In Bologna.

7. Con carta di credito o con bonifico.

With credit card or bank transfer.

8. No, glielo rimborsano completamente se cancella almeno 3 giorni prima.

No, it won't. It will fully refund if she cancels it 3 days before.

9. Le chiede se l'albergo affitta delle macchine.

She asks her if the hotel rents cars.

10. Le consiglia di affittare una bicicletta o un motorino perché i parcheggi costano molto e la macchina è più scomoda.

She suggests she rent a bicycle or a motor scooter because parking costs a lot and the car is less comfortable.

4.7.4 At the restaurant - al ristorante

a./c. customer; b. waiter

a. Buonasera, ho prenotato un tavolo per 2 persone alle 9.

Good evening, I have booked a table for 2 people at 9 o'clock.

b. Buonasera, a che nome?

Good evening, what name?

a. Signora Petrelli.

Mrs. Petrelli.

b. Certamente, mi segua per cortesia. Mentre aspetta, le posso portare qualcosa da bere?

Sure, follow me, please. Could I bring you something to drink while waiting?

a. Si, grazie, una bottiglia di acqua frizzante, per favore.

Yes, please, a bottle of sparkling water, please.

b. Gliela porto subito.

I will bring it immediately.

[arriva l'altro cliente]

[the other client arrives]

a. Ciao, Mattia, ben arrivato. Come stai?

Hi, Mattia, welcome. How are you?

c. Ciao, Carla, bene e tu?

Hi, Carla, fine and you?

a. Bene, grazie. Ordiniamo; che ho molta fame?

Fine thanks. Let's order; I'm very hungry.

c. Certo. Che cosa fanno di buono qui?

Sure. What is good here?

a. Non lo so; è la prima volta che ci vengo. Chiediamo al cameriere.

I do not know; this is the first time I come here. Let's ask the waiter.

b. Siete pronti per ordinare?

Are you ready to order?

a. Si, che cosa ci consiglia?

Yes, what do you suggest?

b. I risotti sono eccezionali; sono le specialità della casa. Oggi fuori menù abbiamo il risotto di zucca con zucchine.

The risottos are excellent; they are the house specialties. Today, off menu, we have pumpkin risotto with zucchini.

a. Per me va bene questo.

This is ok for me.

c. Anche per me.

For me too.

b. Posso portarvi i nostri antipasti misti prima del risotto?

Can I bring you our mixed appetizers before the risotto?

c. Va bene, ma ci porti una sola porzione. Vorrei prendere un secondo dopo.

That's fine, but bring us only one serving. I would like to get a main course after.

b. D'accordo. Volete del vino?

All right. Would you like some wine?

c. Si, rosso per cortesia.

Yes, red please.

b. Ecco qui il vostro antipasto.

Here is your appetizer.

a. Buon appetito!

Enjoy your meal!

c. Anche a te!

You too!

b. Posso portare via?

Can I take everything away?

a. Si, ci potrebbe portare del pane, per favore?

Yes, could you bring us some bread, please?

b. Subito.

Immediately.

c. Il risotto era buonissimo. Ora vorrei ordinare una bistecca.

The risotto was very tasty. Now I would like to order a steak.

b. Ben cotta o al sangue?

Medium or rare?

c. Rare.

b. Vuole anche dell'insalata o delle patate arrosto?

Would you like some salad or roasted potatoes too?

c. Perché no? Un po' di insalata.

Why not, some salad.

c. Ci può portare il conto, per favore?

Can we have the check, please?

b. Ecco qui.

Here you are.

c. Posso pagare con carta di credito?

Can I pay by credit card?

b. Certamente. Ecco qui la sua ricevuta. Arrivederci.

Sure. Here is your receipt. Bye-bye.

a.c. Bye-bye!

4.7.4.1 Questions

1. A che ora aveva prenotato il tavolo Carla?

What time had Carla booked the table?

2. Che cosa ordina Carla mentre aspetta?

What does Carla order while she waits?

3. Qual è la specialità della casa?

What is the house specialty?

4. Che cosa offre il cameriere fuori menù?

What does the waiter offer off menu?

5. Che cosa prendono Mattia e Carla da bere?

What do Mattia and Carla have to drink?

6. Che cosa prendono Mattia e Carla prima del risotto?

What do Mattia and Carla have before the risotto?

7. Com'era il risotto per Mattia?

How was the risotto for Mattia?

8. Che cosa ordina Mattia dopo il risotto?

What does Mattia order after the risotto?

9. Cosa ordina di contorno Mattia?

What does Mattia order as a side dish?

10. Come paga Mattia?

How does Mattia pay?

4.7.4.2 Answer keys

1. Alle 9.

At 9 o'clock.

2. Una bottiglia di acqua frizzante.

A bottle of sparkling water.

3. Il risotto.

The risotto.

4. Risotto alla zucca con zucchine.

Pumpkin risotto with zucchini.

5. Vino rosso.

Red wine.

6. Gli antipasti.

Appetizers.

7. Molto buono.

Very tasty.

8. Una bistecca al sangue.

A rare steak.

9. Dell'insalata.

Some salad.

10. Con carta di credito.

By credit card.

Section 5 – Vocabulary

5.1 Nouns and adjectives - nomi e aggettivi

5.1.1 Nations and nationalities - nazioni e nazionalità

Italia - italiano (Italy - Italian)

Francia - francese (France - French)

Inghilterra - inglese (England - English)

Regno Unito - Britannico (United Kingdom - British)

Irlanda - irlandese (Ireland - Irish)

Germania - tedesco (Germany - German)

Spagna - spagnolo (Spain - Spanish)

Portogallo - portoghese (Portugal - Portuguese)

Stati Uniti - statunitense/americano (United States - American)

Canada - canadese (Canada - Canadian)

Cina - cinese (China - Chinese)

Giappone - giapponese (Japan - Japanese)

Russia - russo (Russia - Russian)

5.1.2 Physical appearance - aspetto fisico

Occhi piccoli/grandi/azzurri/castani/neri/verdi (small/big/blue/brown/black/green eyes)

Capelli lunghi/corti/lisci/ricci/biondi/neri/castani/rossi (long/short/straight/curly/blonde/black/brown/red hair)

Alto/basso (tall/short)

Magro/grasso (thin/fat)

5.1.3. Family – famiglia

Padre/madre (father/mother)

Nonno/nonna (grandfather/grandmother)

Genitori (parents)

Nonni (grandparents)

Parenti (relatives)

Figlio/figlia (son/daughter)

Fratello/sorella (brother/sister)

Zio/zia (uncle/aunt)

Nipote (grandson/granddaughter/nephew/niece)

5.1.4 Jobs – mestieri/lavori

Infermiere (nurse)

Avvocato (lawyer)

Traduttore (translator)

Panettiere (baker)

Macellaio (butcher)

Barista (barman)

Tassista (taxi driver)

Commesso (shop assistant)

Segretario (secretary)

Pompiere (fireman)

Imprenditore (businessman)

Operaio (factory worker)

Cameriere/cameriera (waiter/waitress)

Postino (postman)

Medico/dottore (doctor)

Cuoco (cook)

Poliziotto (policeman)

Impiegato (employee)

Giornalista (journalist)

Idraulico (plumber)

Parrucchiere (hairdresser)

Insegnante (teacher)

5.1.5 Seasons – stagioni

Autunno (fall)

Inverno (winter)

Primavera (spring)

Estate (summer)

5.1.6 Body - corpo

Viso (face)

Occhi (eyes)

Naso (nose)

Bocca (mouth)

Labbra (lips)

Testa (head)

Collo (neck)

Spalla (shoulder)

Braccio/braccia (arm/arms)

Mano (hand)

Gamba (leg)

Piede (foot)

Dito/dita (finger/fingers)

5.1.7 Medical words - parole mediche

Avere (to have got)

Mal di pancia (stomach ache)

Mal di testa (headache)

Mal di denti (toothache)

Mal di gola (sore throat)

Mal di schiena (backache)

Fare male... (to hurt)

Ex. mi fa male la gamba (my leg hurts)

5.1.8 House and furniture - casa e mobilio

Ingresso (entrance)

Salotto (living room)

Sala da pranzo (dining room)

Cucina (kitchen)

Camera da letto (bedroom)

Bagno (bathroom)

Giardino (garden)

Cantina/taverna (basement)

Balcone (balcony)

Terrazzo (terrace)

Soffitta (attic)

Scale (staircase)

Ascensore (elevator)

Pavimento (floor)
Soffitto (ceiling)
Tetto (roof)
Porta (door)
Finestra (window)
Cancello (gate)
Divano (couch)
Poltrona (armchair)
Sedia (chair)
Tavolo (table)
Letto (bed)
Lavandino (sink)
Libreria (bookshelf)
Armadio (wardrobe/closet)
Tappeto (carpet)
Tende (curtains)
Lampada (lamp)
Specchio (mirror)

5.8.1.1 Objects and tools – oggetti e strumenti

[kitchen]

Forchetta (fork)
Coltello (knife)
Cucchiaio (spoon)
Cucchiaino (teaspoon)
Bicchiere (glass)
Tazza (cup)
Tazzina (small cup)

Tovaglia (tablecloth)
Tovagliolo (napkin)
Piatto piano (plate)
Piatto fondo (soup plate)
Fornelli (stove)
Forno (oven)
Frigorifero (fridge)
Congelatore (freezer)
Lavandino (sink)

[bathroom]
Asciugamano (towel)
Accappatoio (bathrobe)
Spazzolino (toothbrush)
Dentifricio (toothpaste)
Spazzola (hairbrush)
Pettine (comb)
Rasoio (razor)
Bagnoschiuma (bath gel)
Docciaschiuma (shower gel)
Asciugacapelli (hair dryer)
Doccia (shower)
Vasca da bagno (bathtub)

[bedroom]
Lenzuolo (sheet)
Coperta (blanket)
Cuscino (pillow)
Pigiama (pyjamas)

5.1.9 In the street - in strada

Strisce pedonali (crosswalk)

Incrocio (intersection)

Semaforo (traffic light)

Ponte (bridge)

Zona pedonale (pedestrian area)

Via (street)

Viale (avenue)

Piazza (square)

Rotonda (rotary)

Corsia dei taxi o degli autobus (taxi or bus lane)

Autostrada (highway)

Fermata dell'autobus, della metro, del tram (tram, subway, and bus stop)

A destra/sinistra (on the right/left)

5.1.10 In the city - in città

Chiesa (church)

Ufficio postale (postal office)

Scuola (school)

Comune (town hall)

Supermercato (supermarket)

Mercato (market)

Ristorante (restaurant)

Albergo (hotel)

Parco giochi (playground)

Libreria (bookshop)

Farmacia (drugstore)

Fruttivendolo (fruit seller)

Gioielleria (jewelry shop)

Macelleria (butcher shop)

Panificio (bakery)

Fioraio (flower shop)

5.1.11 Clothes and accessories – abbigliamento e accessori

Maglione (sweater)

Orecchini (earrings)

Occhiali da vista/da sole (eye/sunglasses)

Scarpe (shoes)

Calze (socks)

Collana (necklace)

Camicia (shirt)

Gonna (skirt)

Sciarpa (scarf)

Anello (ring)

Stivali (boots)

Guanti (gloves)

Cintura (belt)

Bracciale (bracelet)

Pantaloni (trousers)

Cappotto (coat)

Cappello (hat)

Tuta (track suit)

Costume da bagno (swim suit)

Vestito/abito da donna/uomo (dress/suit)

Maglietta (T-shirt)

Giacca (jacket)

5.1.12 The Weather - il meteo/tempo

Che tempo fa? (what's the weather like?)

Piove (it rains)

Nevica (it snows)

C'è il sole/è soleggiato (it is sunny)

C'è vento/è ventilato (it is windy)

Ci sono le nuvole/è nuvoloso (it is cloudy)

C'è nebbia (it is foggy)

Fa caldo (it is hot)

Fa freddo (it is cold)

C'è umidità/è umido (it is wet)

La pioggia (the rain)

La neve (the snow)

Il sole (the sun)

La nebbia (the fog)

Il vento (the wind)

5.1.13 Feelings and emotions - sentimenti ed emozioni

arrabbiato (angry)

rabbia (anger)

contento/felice (happy)

felicità (happiness)

deluso (disappointed)

delusione (disappointment)

imbarazzato (embarrassed)

imbarazzo (embarrassment)

orgoglioso (proud)

orgoglio (pride)

triste (sad)

tristezza (sadness)

timido (shy)

timidezza (shyness)

5.1.14 The environment – l'ambiente

Mare (sea)

Spiaggia (beach)

Costa (coast/shore)

Montagna (mountain)

Collina (hill)

Fiume (river)

Lago (lake)

Cascata (waterfall)

Deserto (desert)

Foresta (forest)

Giungla (jungle)

5.1.15 Means of transport – mezzi di trasporto

Macchina/automobile (car)

Motorino (motor-scooter)

Moto (motorbike)

Bicicletta/bici (bicycle/bike)

Barca (boat)

Nave (ship)

Traghetto (ferry)

Camion (truck)

Tir (lorry)

Aereo (airplane)

Elicottero (helicopter)

5.1.16 Animals – animali

5.1.16.1 In the farm – nella fattoria

Mucca (cow)

Toro (bull)

Maiale (pig)

Pecora (ship)

Cavallo (horse)

Asino (donkey)

Gallina (hen)

Gallo (rooster)

Coniglio (rabbit)

5.1.16.2. Pets – animali domestici

Cane (dog)

Gatto (cat)

Pesce rosso (goldfish)

Criceto (hamster)

5.1.16.3 Wild animals – animali selvatici

Scimmia (monkey)

Squalo (shark)

Lupo (wolf)

Giraffa (giraffe)

Cammello (camel)

Gufo (owl)

Tigre (tiger)

Orso (bear)

Balena (whale)

Leone (lion)

Coccodrillo (crocodile)

Delfino (dolphin)

Elefante (elephant)

Scoiattolo (squirrel)

Serpente (snake)

Canguro (kangaroo)

Volpe (fox)

Pipistrello (bat)

Rana (frog)

Topo (mouse)

5.1.17. Food - cibo

5.1.17.1 Vegetables - verdure

Carciofo (artichoke)

Spinaci (spinach)

Piselli (peas)

Aglio (garlic)

Cipolla (onion)

Zucca (pumpkin)

Funghi (mushrooms)

Sedano (celery)

Melanzana (eggplant)

Carota (carrot)

Patata (potato)

Pomodoro (tomato)

Fagioli (beans)

Fagiolini (green beans)

Peperone (pepper)

Zucchina (zucchini)

Lattuga (lettuce)

5.1.17.2. Fruits – frutta

Fico (fig)

Pesca (peach)

Ananas (pineapple)

Oliva (olive)

Banana (banana)

Anguria (watermelon)

Mela (apple)

Castagne (chestnuts)

Fragola (strawberry)

Grappolo d'uva (grapes)

Cocco (coconut)

Noccioline (peanuts)

Noce (walnut)

Mais (corn)

Limone (lemon)

Arancia (orange)

Ciliegia (cherry)

Albicocca (apricot)

5.1.17.3. Meat – carne

Pollo (chicken)

Manzo (beef)

Agnello (lamb)

Maiale (pork)

Tacchino (turkey)

Anatra (duck)

Bistecca (steak)

Salsiccia (sausage)

Prosciutto (ham)

Pancetta (bacon)

5.1.17.4 Fish and seafood – pesce e frutti di mare

Meluzzo (cod)

Salmone (salmon)

Tonno (tuna)

Polpo (octopus)

Gambero (shrimp)

Cozze (mussels)

Ostrica (oyster)

Aragosta (lobster)

Granchio (crab)

Sardina/acciuga (sardine)

5.1.17.5. Dairy foods – latticini

Formaggio (cheese)

Burro (butter)

Panna (cream)

Latte (milk)

Parmigiano (parmesan cheese)

5.1.17.6. Others – altri

Pane (bread)

Maionese (mayonnaise)

Olio (oil)
Sale (salt)
Pepe (pepper)
Gelato (ice cream)
Uovo/uova (egg/eggs)
Patatine fritte (French fries)
Patate al forno (baked potatoes)
Pasta (pasta)
Zuppa (soup)
Riso (rice)
Polpette (meatballs)
Ciambella (donut)
Biscotti (cookies)
Torta (pie)

5.1.18. Colors – colori

Arancione (orange)
Argento (silver)
Azzurro (light blue)
Bianco (white)
Blu (blue)
Dorato (golden)
Giallo (yellow)
Grigio (gray)
Marrone (brown)
Nero (black)
Rosa (pink)
Rosso (red)

Verde (green)

Viola (purple)

Chiaro (light)

Scuro (dark)

Pallido (pale)

5.1.19. Sports – sport

Atletica (athletics)

Calcio (soccer)

Canotaggio (rowing)

Ciclismo (cycling)

Equitazione (horse riding)

Ginnastica (gym)

Nuoto (swimming)

Pallacanestro (basketball)

Pallavolo (volleyball)

Pugilato (boxing)

Sci (ski)

5.1.20 Italian holidays – festività italiane

1 novembre, Ognissanti – November 1st, All Saints' Day

(in the past, this was a Catholic feast, but nowadays, it's only a day to relax after Halloween night and to realize that winter is coming)

8 dicembre, Immacolata Concezione – December 8th, Immaculate Conception

(historically, it represents the day when Mary became pregnant through the holy spirit; now it is a day dedicated to Christmas decorations and marks the countdown to Christmas holidays)

25 dicembre, Giorno di Natale – December 25th, Christmas Day

26 dicembre, Santo Stefano – December 26th, the day after Christmas

1 gennaio, Capodanno – January 1st, New Year's Day

6 gennaio, Epifania – January 1st, Epiphany

(it is a small version of Christmas; an ugly old woman puts sweeties and candies inside socks. It marks the end of Christmas holidays)

Pasqua – Easter Sunday

Pasquetta – Easter Monday

25 aprile, Festa della Liberazione – April 25th, Liberation Day

(this day commerates the end of Nazi occupation of the country during World War II and the victory of the resistance)

1 maggio, Festa del Lavoro – May 1st, Labor Day

2 giugno, Festa della Repubblica – June 2nd, Republic Day

(when Italy signed the democratic republic system after a Fascist government)

15 agosto, Ferragosto – August 15th

(before it was a Catholic feast, but now represents the highest peak of summer holidays; at night, people watch the sky to see falling stars)

5.1.21 Parts of the car – parti della macchina

Sportello/portiera (door)

Volante (steering wheel)

Cintura di sicurezza (safety belt)

Cruscotto (dashboard)

Contachilometri (odometer)

Leva del cambio (gear level)

Cambio automatico (automatic transmission)

Freno (brake)

Acceleratore (throttle)

Pneumatico/ruota (tyre)

Serbatoio benzina/carburante (fuel tank)

Specchietto retrovisore (rearview mirror)

Specchietto laterale (side-view mirror)

Fanale anteriore/posteriore (headlight/tailight)

Sedile (car seat)

Indicatore direzione/freccia (turn signal)

Parabrezza (windshield)

Tergicristallo (wiper)

5.2 Most commons verbs – verbi più comuni

Accendere (to switch on)

[past participle "acceso"]

Accettare (to accept)

Aggiustare (to fix)

Aiutare (to help)

Alzarsi (to wake up)

Amare (to love)

Aprire (to open)

[past participle "aperto"]

Andare (to go)

[presente indicative "io vado, tu vai, egli/ella va, noi andiamo, voi andate, loro vanno]

Arrivare (to arrive)

Ascoltare (to listen)

Aspettare (to wait)

Attraversare (to cross)

Aver bisogno di (to need)

Avere caldo (to be hot)

Avere fame (to be hungry)

Avere freddo (to be cold)

Avere paura (to be scared)

Avere ragione (to be right)

Avere sete (to be thirsty)

Avere sonno (to be tired)

Avere torto (to be wrong)

Ballare (to dance)

Bere (to drink)

[presente indicative "io bevo, tu bevi, egli/ella beve, noi beviamo, voi bevete, loro bevono]

Bollire (to boil)

Cadere (to fall)

Cambiare (to change)

Camminare (to walk)

Cancellare (to cancel)

Cantare (to sing)

Capire (to understand)

[presente indicative "io capisco, tu capisci, egli/ella capisce, noi capiamo, voi capite, loro capiscono]

Cenare (to have dinner)

Chiamare (to call)

Chiedere (to ask)

[past participle "chiesto"]

Chiudere (to close)

[past participle "chiuso"]

Cominciare (to begin)

Comprare (to buy)

Contare (to count)

Correre (to run)

[past participle "corso"]

Costare (to cost)

Costruire (to build)

[presente indicative "io costruisco, tu costruisci, egli/ella costruisce, noi costruiamo, voi costruite, loro costruiscono]

Credere (to believe)

Crescere (to grow)

[presente indicative "io cresco, tu cresci, egli/ella cresce, noi cresciamo, voi crescete, loro crescono]

[past participle "cresciuto"]

Cuocere (to cook)

[presente indicative "io cuocio, tu cuoci, egli/ella cuoce, noi cuociamo, voi cuocete, loro cuociono]

[past participle "cotto"]

Dare (to give)

[presente indicative "io do, tu dai, egli/ella dà, noi diamo, voi date, loro danno]

Dare una festa (to have a party)

Decidere (to decide)

[past participle "deciso"]

Dimenticare (to forget)

Dire (to say/to tell)

[presente indicative "io dico, tu dici, egli/ella dice, noi diciamo, voi dite, loro dicono]

[past participle "detto"]

Diventare (to become)

Divertirsi (to have fun)

Dormire (to sleep)

Entrare (to get in)

Fare (to do/to make)

[presente indicative "io faccio, tu fai, egli/ella fa, noi facciamo, voi fate, loro fanno]

[past participle "fatto"]

Fare colazione (to have breakfast)

Farsi la barba (to shave)

Farsi la doccia/il bagno (to have a shower/a bath)

Fare un riposino (to have a nap)

Fermarsi (to stop)

Finire (to finish/to end)

[presente indicative "io finisco, tu finisci, egli/ella finisce, noi finiamo, voi finite, loro finiscono]

Fumare (to smoke)

Giocare (to play)

Girare (to turn)

Guardare (to look)

Guidare (to drive)

Imparare (to learn)

Incontrare/conoscere (to meet)

[presente indicative "io conosco, tu conisci, egli/ella conosce, noi conosciamo, voi conoscete, loro conscono]

[past participle "conosciuto"]

Indossare (to wear)

Insegnare (to teach)

Iscriversi (to sign up/to register/to enroll)

Lasciare (to let/to leave)

Lavare (to wash)

Lavorare (to work)

Leggere (to read)

[past participle "letto"]

Mangiare (to eat)

Mandare (to send)

Mescolare (to stir)

Morire (to die)

[presente indicative "io muoio, tu muori, egli/ella muore, noi moriamo, voi morite, loro muoiono]

[past participle "morto"]

Nascere (to be born)

[presente indicative "io nasco, tu nasci, egli/ella nasce, noi nasciamo, voi nascete, loro nascono]

[past participle "nato"]

Nuotare (to swim)

Offrire (to offer)

[presente indicative "io offro, tu offri, egli/ella offre, noi offriamo, voi offrite, loro offrono]

[past participle "offerto"]

Ordinare (to order)

Pagare (to pay)

Parlare (to speak)

Partire (to leave)

Passare (to pass by)

Pensare (to think)

Perdere/Mancare (to lose/to miss)

[past participle "perso"]

Pettinare (to comb)

Portare (to bring)

Pranzare (to have lunch)

Prendere (to take)

[past participle "preso"]

Preoccuparsi (to worry)

Preparare (to prepare)

Pulire (to clean)

[presente indicative "io pulisco, tu pulisci, egli/ella pulisce, noi puliamo, voi pulite, loro puliscono]

Restare (to stay)

[past participle "rimasto"]

Ricevere (to receive)

Ricordare (to remember)

Ridere (to laugh)

[past participle "riso"]

Riempire (to fill)

Rispondere (to answer/to reply)

[past participle "risposto"]

Ritornare (to come back)

Rompere (to brake)

[past participle "rotto"]

Rubare (to steal)

Salire (to come up)

[presente indicative "io salgo, tu sali, egli/ella sale, noi saliamo, voi salite, loro salgono]

Scegliere (to choose)

[presente indicative "io scelgo, tu scegli, egli/ella sceglie, noi scegliamo, voi scegliete, loro scelgono]

[past participle "scelto"]

Scendere (to climb down/to get off)

[past participle "sceso"]

Scrivere (to write)

[past participle "scritto"]

Sembrare (to look like/ to seem like)

Sentire/provare (to feel)

Sentire (to hear)

Significare (to mean)

Sollevare (to lift)

Sparire (to disappear)

[presente indicative "io sparisco, tu sparisci, egli/ella sparisce, noi spariamo, voi sparite, loro spariscono]

Spegnere (to switch off)

[presente indicative "io spengo, tu spegni, egli/ella spegne, noi spegniamo, voi spegnete, loro spengono]

[past participle "spento"]

Spendere/trascorrere (to spend)

[past participle "speso/trascorso"]

Spiegare (to exaplain)

Spostare (to move)

Studiare (to study)

Suonare (to ring/to play)

Tagliare (to cut)

Telefonare (to phone)

Tenere (to hold/to keep)

[presente indicative "io tengo, tu tieni, egli/ella tiene, noi teniamo, voi tenete, loro tengono]

Tradurre (to translate)

[past participle "tradotto"]

Traslocare (to move – "to change place")

Trovare (to find)

Truccarsi (to put on makeup)

Usare (to use)

Uscire (to go out)

[presente indicative "io esco, tu esci, egli/ella esce, noi usciamo, voi uscite, loro escono]

Vedere (to see/to watch)

[past participle "visto"]

Vendere (to sell)

Venire (to come)

[presente indicative "io vengo, tu vieni, egli/ella viene, noi veniamo, voi venite, loro vengono]

Vestirsi (to get dressed)

Viaggiare (to travel)

Vincere (to win)

[past participle "vinto"]

Vivere (to live)

[past participle "vissuto"]

Volare (to fly)

Conclusion

Whatever your reason for learning Italian, this book should have been useful and provided you with the basic tools to be able to explain yourself and understand an elementary conversation.

The first two sections explained basic grammar rules, comparing them with the English language, which should have given you both an aid to learning them easily shown you how important the grammar is. In fact, even if it could be considered something "technical" by many, something reserved for "experts", it actually gives you tools to manage words and phrases so that you can communicate efficiently in any situation.

The third section gave you the chance to test yourself by putting into practice what you learned in sections 1 and 2 and to go back to those sections if there was something you didn't get right.

As stated in the introduction, the main aim of a language is communication. And what is very important and essential is to understand and to be understood everywhere by everyone. Section 4 showed you how Italian grammar rules are used in real and common situations, "how they work" in practice. As suggested, you should have tried to replicate dialogues pretending to be one of the characters involved, and this is something you should carry on doing to improve your language level, and also by changing the sentences and words.

Language is still an ordered mix of words that translate what is in your mind, what you are thinking, and what you want to say. Thus, the function of the last section was to give you essential words and basic expressions so you can express yourself on any occasion.

Of course, the path is long. There are still many aspects, grammar rules, tenses, words, and expressions of the Italian language that you didn't learn in this book, but these four sections have certainly given you the basic tools, which represent a good starting point!

Remember, learning a language is an endless journey. During it, you will encounter difficulties, but don't be discouraged! In the end, you will be rewarded with the most exciting prize: the knowledge of a new language. And this means the opportunity to communicate and express yourself to and with other people, and to get into a new culture, having the possibility to understand it from an inner point of view.

Part 2: Mastering Italian Words

Increase Your Vocabulary with Over 200 Crucial Words in Context and Over 1000 Sentences

Introduction

Would you like to improve your Italian but do not like grammar? Would you like to study Italian but have already tried classic methods and want a different approach? Well, this is the book you need. In fact, for those who already have some concept of Italian, this guide offers you a wide range of words to refresh your grammar rules and help you learn the meaning of different words and how they change depending on the context. On the other hand, for those who want an innovative and dynamic approach to Italian, this manual offers you the opportunity to deduce grammar, including different tense uses. Therefore, you have the chance to learn lots of words, which is needed while learning a new language.

If you are asking yourself if this method is actually useful or not, consider that it represents a new modern learning system, which includes an active memorizing and review process, using metacognition. This explanation may not sound immediate, so here is how it works.

This method is based on the idea that grammar rules are not presented as abstract but used in their natural context. And if you think that the main purpose of a language is to be spoken, what would be better than working directly with words?

As often proposed by schools and language courses, grammar is a set of rules that require the learner to memorize the names of special linguistic categories. However, if you think about a language in its meta-linguistic definition, there is more in the learning process: terms, notions, topics, and the language itself. Classic learning models are based on meta-linguistic definitions, which are never used when a person learns a language—only when listening to it, as children do. To make it easier: you do not need an article to be called as such, as the most important thing is to know how to use it. So, targeting and studying linguistic definitions is a waste of time, especially if your goal is to have a basic knowledge of a language so that you can speak it in a reasonable time, putting aside years and years of studying.

Thus, memorizing words via this book's process is simpler, as you can always use the sentences you learn by recalling the words you need. This is how you get the chance to learn Italian fast, enjoying your learning process much more than you would if you used the classic methods. Step by step, sentence by sentence, word by word, you will find yourself more and more comfortable with the language. This is the dynamic immersion method, which is based on how kids learn their mother tongue. But it is also built on how the brain works to memorize. The brain is a huge net of neurons linked with each other, creating thousands of links and combinations that characterize memory. The more links and combinations your neurons have, the more things you will memorize. The more associations you create with words, images, or translations into your language, the more you will remember them. Also, never forget that your brain's storage capability is always much larger than a computer's. So, nothing stops you from learning languages.

Each word and sentence is translated step by step, and this is because translation—together with oral comprehension, conversation, and grammar—is one of the most significant and common tools used by language teachers, tutors, and manuals. This guide is not meant to give you the tools you will need to translate texts—which is part of another type of tutoring and education. The purpose of translations here is to show you how words, concepts, and expressions are proposed in another language that is not your mother tongue. And, again, it is supposed to be learned in context, not from rules.

Sentences propose not only grammar focuses that determine how to build a sentence and how to use pronouns, prepositions, and verbs, but also particular words, which differ for sounds and letters. Of course, you will find that all words have many meanings (i.e., ideas or objects linked to that word), or change meaning depending on the context. Moreover, sentences themselves are easy but are always written as a native speaker would write them. The translations given try to follow the natural flow and used expressions of English, and are literal so that making a correspondence—a link between the two languages—does not represent hard work for learners, who are reading this book without the tutoring of a teacher. So, sentences appear to be true, created by a spontaneous speaker. At each point, you will find a focus on particular words, but this does not mean that those are the only elements you can get from it. On the contrary, many other important elements will be useful for learning purposes. As mentioned, the structure is easy but can be repetitive. This should help you get the meaning more easily and faster without facing too many difficulties from sentence to sentence.

You may be thinking that learning Italian from a list of sentences could be not useful when you find yourself talking to a native speaker because they go off the "beaten track." However, this book contains a list of beneficial sentences that show you how words work in different contexts. And the context is what will provide you a way to get through the communication system, avoiding misunderstandings linked to the fact that you may have missed a word.

Now, it is time to move on and learn how to use this guide.

Supposing that you have already studied Italian—even just a bit—what you will have to do is read the title containing the words and try and memorize them using the translations proposed. Then, read the sentences one by one. At the end of each reading, focus on the translation, and revise all the grammar rules. Now, you should be ready to view words and create a sentence on your own. If you have never studied Italian before, do not worry. The steps are the same, except for the grammar rule revision one. In this case, you should pay it more attention and try to focus on what grammar rule is used and how it works.

If you read the book from the beginning to the end following these steps, you will finish it with a wider and more general knowledge of Italian words. If you don't have time to follow all the steps, feel free to only focus on some points. Another advantage of this learning method is that there is no need to be afraid to skip some parts, as there's no set line or path to follow. Hence, technically, you could randomly open the book and keep studying it for years and years. This book is not an educational manual; it is a source you can use in any way you want.

Do not be afraid of approaching the study of a new language. This guide's main purpose is to show you a new and easier way to learn Italian. Polyglots have been beginners many times, but they all say that what really matters in the learning process is memorizing and using words. Also, you do not need to become high proficiency immediately—it takes time and practice to become fluent. You can express yourself in many contexts and on many topics without being excellent.

Lastly, remember that mastering another language represents one of the most interesting challenges and opportunities that you will have, as it exposes you to a wide range of experiences!

1. avere – to have

Ho molta fame, ho sete e ho anche sonno! È stato un giorno molto stancante!

I am hungry, I am thirsty, and I am also tired! It has been a really tiring day!

Ho fretta e non ti posso spiegare perché tu hai torto e io ragione.

I am in a hurry, and I can't explain why you are wrong and why I am right.

Mi succede una cosa strana: d'estate ho freddo e d'inverno ho caldo.

There is a weird thing that happens to me: I am cold during summer and hot during winter.

Luca ha un cane e un gatto che vanno d'accordo.

Luca has got a dog and a cat who get along well.

2. fare – to do/to make

Mi piace fare il bagno di sera e fare la doccia di mattina, prima di fare colazione. Lo faccio da quando sono bambina.

I like taking a bath in the evening and taking a shower in the morning, right before breakfast. I have been doing it since I was a child.

Tutti i bambini fanno un riposino dopo pranzo.

All children take a nap after lunch.

Mentre Marco fa i compiti, sua madre fa una torta.

While Marco is doing his homework, his mother is making a cake.

3. abbastanza – enough

Non ci sono abbastanza posti per tutti in macchina. Tu e Roberto dovete prendere il treno.

There are not enough seats in the car for you all. You and Roberto have to take the train.

4. troppo – too much

Abbiamo mangiato troppo, e ora mi fa male lo stomaco.

We have eaten too much, and now I have got a stomachache.

5. cioè – it is to say

Questa squadra, cioè il Milan, è il nostro team preferito.

This team, called Milan, is our favorite one.

6. che – that/what/which

Il mio capo dice sempre che non dobbiamo lavorare nel weekend, ma ogni settimana mi chiede di lavorare sia di sabato che di domenica.

My boss always says that we do not have to work at weekends, but every week he asks me to work on both Saturday and Sunday.

Che film avete visto ieri al cinema?

What movie did you see yesterday, at the cinema?

Il padre di Mario, che è appena entrato da quella porta, è un avvocato.

Mario's father, who has just come in from that door, is a lawyer.

7. chi – who

Chi è quel ragazzo davanti all'ascensore? Mi sembra di conoscerlo.

Who is that boy in front of the lift? I think I know him.

8. futuro – future

Non sappiamo cosa succederà in futuro, ma io sono sicuro che vivrò su una spiaggia tropicale.

We don't know what will happen in the future, but I am sure I will live on a tropical beach.

9. lavare/lavarsi – to wash/ to clean

Tutte le settimane lavo la macchina, la voglio sempre pulita.

Every week, I wash my car. I want it to be always clean.

Luca si lava sempre prima di fare colazione.

Luca always washes himself before having breakfast.

Non è facile lavarsi i capelli se sono molto lunghi. Ci vuole molto tempo.

It's not easy to wash your hair if it is very long. It takes a lot of time.

10. chiamare/chiamarsi – to call/to be named (my name is . . .)

Dovete chiamare tutti i vostri amici e dire loro che la festa si farà alle 5 del pomeriggio e non alle 6, come avevo detto prima.

You have to call all of your friends and tell them the party will be at 5:00 p.m., and not at 6:00, as I said earlier.

11. rompere/rompersi – to break/to break a bone of your body/to break down

Non giocate con il pallone in casa! Romperete un altro vaso!

Don't play ball inside the house! You will break another vase.

Giorgio non giocherà con noi questo sabato perché si è rotto una gamba giocando a tennis.

Giorgio won't play with us this Saturday, because he broke his leg playing tennis.

La macchina di mia madre si è rotta di nuovo e devo prendere l'autobus per andare a scuola.

My mother's car has broken down again, and I have to take the bus to get to school.

12. sbagliare/sbagliarsi – to make a mistake/ to be wrong

Ragazzi mi dispiace, ma avete sbagliato strada. Il mercato è dall'altra parte della città.

Sorry, guys, but you have made a mistake. The market is on the other side of the city.

Pensavo che non ci fossero più biglietti e invece mi sbagliavo.

I thought there were no tickets left, but I was wrong.

13. alzare/alzarsi – to lift/to wake up/to stand up

Potresti alzare tu quella scatola? Mi fa male la schiena.

Could you please lift that box? My back hurts.

Tutte le mattine devo alzarmi alle 5 e devo andare al lavoro.

Every morning, I have to wake up at 5:00 a.m. and commute to work.

Tutti quelli che hanno già ricevuto i premi potrebbero alzarsi in piedi?

Those of you who have received their prizes, could you please stand up?

14. chiedere/chiedersi – to ask/to wonder

Mi scusi, vorrei chiedere se posso avere un altro bicchiere di vino rosso?

Sorry, I would like to ask you if I may have another glass of red wine?

Eccoti! Ci stavamo chiedendo dove fossi.

Here you are! We were wondering where you were.

15. piacere– to like/nice to meet you/pleasure/favor

A Maria piace molto camminare sulla spiaggia con il cane.

Maria really enjoys walking on the beach with her dog.

Ciao, io sono Giulia, piacere.

Hi, I am Giulia. Nice to meet you.

Mangiare il gelato è sempre un piacere.

Eating ice cream is always a pleasure.

La zia mi ha chiesto di farle un favore: badare ai miei cugini sabato sera.

Aunt asked me to do her a favor and look after my cousins on Saturday night.

16. Moglie/marito– wife/husband

Dopo che Luigi e Marta si sono sposati, sono diventati marito e moglie e ora sono molto felici.

After Luigi and Maria got married, they became husband and wife. They are very happy.

17. zitto – silent/shut up

Suo figlio è un ragazzo molto tranquillo, sta sempre in silenzio e fa il suo dovere.

Your son is a very quiet boy. He always keeps silent while doing his duty.

Zitto per favore! Non riesco a sentire il telegiornale.

Shut up, please! I can't hear the TV news.

18. febbre – fever/temperature

Ho la febbre da tre giorni, e non riesco ad alzarmi dal letto.

I have had a fever for three days, and I can't leave my bed.

19. imparare – to learn

Mi piace molto imparare l'italiano, e questo mi aiuterà la prossima estate, quando andrò in vacanza in Italia.

I like learning Italian a lot, and this will help me next summer, when I will go on holiday to Italy.

20. utile/inutile – useful/worthless

Questo attrezzo è molto utile per preparare la carne al barbecue.

This tool is very useful to cook meat with the barbeque.

Ogni nostro tentativo è stato inutile. Abbiamo perso una grande opportunità lavorativa.

Every single one of our efforts has been worthless. We have lost a great job opportunity.

21. essere/stare – to be/to stay

Sono le 9 e siamo già tutti al lavoro.

It's 9 o'clock, and we are all already at work.

Questo fine settimana piove e stiamo a casa.

It will rain this weekend and we will stay at home.

È da qualche giorno che non sto bene. Dovrei rimanere a letto e riposare.

I haven't felt well for a few days. I should stay in bed and rest.

Stai attento! Quello scalino è molto alto.

Be careful! That step is very high.

Sta a te, tira i dadi!

You're up! Roll the dice!

Questo albergo è magnifico, mi sembra di stare in paradiso.

This hotel is wonderful. It feels like heaven.

Sto ancora mangiando, possiamo sentirci più tardi?

I'm still eating. Can we talk later?

22. sentire/sentirci – to feel/to hear

Tutti si sentono meglio quando sono fortunati.

People feel better when they are lucky.

È arrivata la primavera! Sento gli uccellini che cantano.

Spring has come! I can hear birds singing.

Purtroppo sto invecchiando e non ci sento molto bene.

Unfortunately, I am getting old, and I can't hear very well.

23. anche/ancora – also-too/still-again

Stasera alla festa c'è anche Marco, non lo sopporto.

Tonight, at the party, Marco will come too. I can't stand him.

Anche questo è da aggiungere alla lista delle cose da fare per il matrimonio.

This is also to be added to the to-do list for the wedding.

Sono le 6 di sera e stiamo ancora lavorando.

It's 6:00 p.m., and we are still working.

Scusami ancora, non volevo essere maleducato.

Once again, I'm sorry. I didn't want to be rude.

24. fiore – flower

Luca mi ha portato un mazzo di fiori per il mio compleanno; è stato molto gentile.

Luca got me a bouquet of flowers for my birthday; he was very kind.

Ciao, Sonia! Sono anni che non ci vediamo, sei un fiore!

Hi, Sonia! Long time no see. You look great!

25. vivere/abitare – to live

Abitiamo in questa casa da tre anni, mentre prima abitavamo in un appartamento più piccolo, a nord della città.

We have lived here for three years. Beforehand, we lived in a smaller flat in the north of the city.

Viviamo in Francia da quando siamo bambini.

We have been living in France since we were children.

26. vita – life/waist

La vita per tanti è molto difficile.

For many people, life is very hard.

Ciao, Marco! Come stai? È una vita che non ci vediamo.

Hi, Marco! How are you? Long time no see.

Questa gonna è bella, ma mi dà fastidio sulla vita.

This skirt is beautiful, but it is uncomfortable on the waist.

27. mezzo – medium/mean/half

Il giornale è un mezzo per trasmettere informazioni.

The newspaper is a way of spreading information.

L'autobus non è il mezzo di trasporto più rapido per girare in città.

The bus isn't the fastest means of transport to go round the city.

È tardi! Sono le tre e mezzo e lo spettacolo inizia alle 4!

It's late! It's half past three, and the show starts at 4:00 p.m.!

28. antico/vecchio – ancient/old

Il porto di Genova è molto antico. È uno dei più antichi in Italia.

The port of Genoa is very ancient. It's one of the most ancient in Italy.

Chi è il più vecchio della tua famiglia? Sicuramente mio nonno: ha 98 anni.

Who's the eldest member of your family? It's indeed my grandfather: he is 98 years old.

29. accendere/spegnere – to switch on/to switch off

Quando vai a dormire, devi spegnere il cellulare. Io lo spengo sempre la sera e lo accendo di nuovo al mattino.

When you go to sleep, you have to switch off your cell phone. I always switch it off at night, and switch it on again in the morning.

30. dolce/amaro – sweet/bitter

Alcuni italiani bevono il caffè dolce e altri amaro. La tradizione del caffè però dice che andrebbe bevuto senza zucchero.

Some Italians drink sweet coffee, and others drink it bitter. But tradition says it should be drunk without sugar.

31. c'è/ci sono – there is/are

Ho deciso di fare una torta, ma non ci sono uova. Dobbiamo comprarle. Però, abbiamo della farina e del cioccolato.

I have decided to make a cake, but there aren't any eggs. We need to buy them. We have some flour and some chocolate, though.

32. posso/potrei – Can I/could I

Mamma, posso uscire con i miei amici? Mi hanno chiamato e mi hanno chiesto di andare con loro.

Mom, can I go out with my friends? They called me and asked me to go with them.

Mi scusi, potrei avere il conto? E potrei avere anche un caffè, per favore?

Excuse me, may I have the bill? And may I have one coffee as well, please?

33. madre/padre-zia/zio-sorella/fratello – mother/father-aunt/uncle-sister/brother

Mia madre ha una sorella e un fratello, e mio padre solo un fratello. Quindi, ho due zii e una zia.

My mother has got one sister and one brother, and my father only one brother. So, I have two uncles and one aunt.

34. animale – animal

Ci sono molti tipi di animali: gli animali domestici vivono in casa, gli animali da allevamento vivono nella fattoria, e gli animali selvatici vivono nella foresta.

There are many types of animals: pets live in the house, farm animals live in a farm, and wild animals live in the forest.

35. mai – ever/never

Sei mai andato al mare con la pioggia?

Have you ever gone to the beach on a rainy day?

Molte persone non hanno mai capito quanto sia importante leggere.

Many people have never understood how important it is to read.

36. più ... di – more ... than

Mia sorella è più grande di me. Lei ha 47 anni, e io 43.

My sister is older than me. She is 47 years, and I am 43.

37. meno ... di – less ... than

Luca è meno alto di Michele ma è anche meno magro.

Luca is less tall than Michele but is also less thin.

38. come – as ... as

La torta che ho preparato è buona come quella di mia madre.

The cake I have baked is as tasty as my mother's.

39. migliore – better

Lui è sicuramente una persona migliore quando è con i suoi amici.

He sure is a better person when he is with his friends.

40. peggiore – worse

Questo ristorante è peggiore di quello dove siamo stati ieri sera. Non ho mangiato nulla!

This restaurant is worse than the one we went to yesterday. I've eaten nothing!

41. il più – the most

La tua macchina non è la più veloce sul mercato, ma è la più comoda!

Your car is not the fastest on the market, but it's the most comfortable!

42. il migliore – the best

Questo è il film migliore che abbia mai visto.

This is the best movie I have ever seen.

43. il peggiore – the worst

Questa è stata l'esperienza peggiore della nostra vita. Non torneremo mai più in questo albergo!

This was the worst experience of our life. We will never come back to this hotel!

44. . . . issimo/a – very...

Ieri sera, Mario ha conosciuto una ragazza bellissima, ma ha perso il suo numero di cellulare.

Yesterday night, Mario met a very beautiful girl, but he lost her phone number.

45. in/a – in/to

Vivo a Milano, ma per il mio lavoro, vado spesso a Torino. Viaggio molto, e una volta al mese, vado in Germania, a Monaco.

I live in Milan, but for my job, I often go to Turin. I travel a lot, and once a month, I go to Munich, Germany.

L'estate prossima, andiamo in vacanza in Sicilia, a Palermo. Andremo anche a Salina, una piccola isola nell'arcipelago delle Eolie.

Next summer, we are going on holiday to Palermo. We are also going to Salina, a small island in the Eolie archipelago.

La famiglia di Alessandro vive in Argentina, infatti vanno spesso a Buenos Aires a trovarla. Loro però non sono mai stati in Italia.

Alessandro's family lives in Argentina. In fact, they often go to Buenos Aires to visit it, but they have never been to Italy.

46. a – to

Posso dare questo libro a Maria così te lo può portare a scuola domani se ti serve.

I can give Maria this book so she can bring it to you at school tomorrow if you need it.

47. di – of

Questa è la casa di mia sorella.

This is my sister's house.

La mensa della scuola è al primo piano.

The school canteen is on the first floor.

Questo è un tavolo in legno.

This is a wooden table.

48. di/da – from

Lucia è di Milano, ma i suoi amici vengono dalla Puglia e sono di Taranto.

Lucia is from Milan, but her friends come from Apulia and are from Taranto.

49. con – with/by

Mio padre viene sempre con me alle partite di calcio, anche se non gli piace questo sport.

My father always comes with me to soccer matches, even if he does not like this sport.

Vado spesso a Milano con il treno perché è molto veloce, ma se devo andare a Bologna ci vado con la macchina perché ci mette meno tempo.

I often go to Milan by train because it is faster, but if I have to go to Bologna, I go there by car because it takes less time.

Non riesco a tagliare la carne con questo coltello, devo usarne un altro.

I can't cut the meat with this knife. I'll have to use another one.

50. su – on/over/about

Il vaso di fiori sul tavolo è molto bello; lo ha fatto mia nonna quando era giovane.

The flower pot on the table is very beautiful. My grandmother made it when she was young.

Gli aerei volano sulla città, e spesso il rumore che fanno spaventa il mio gatto. Non è un gatto coraggioso.

Airplanes fly over the city, and the noise they make scares my cat. It's not a brave cat.

La professoressa ci ha detto che dobbiamo preparare una tesina sulla Seconda Guerra Mondiale, concentrandoci su un argomento che ci piace, e poi caricarla sulla piattaforma online della scuola.

Our professor told us that we have to write an essay on War World II, focusing on a topic we like and then upload it onto the online school platform.

51. for – per

Luigi e Maria sono partiti per la loro luna di miele.

Luigi and Maria left for their honeymoon.

Tutto quello che faccio, lo faccio per te.

All I do, I do it for you.

Non buttare le cose per terra! Smettila di inquinare!

Do not throw trash on the ground! Stop polluting!

Per favore, potresti chiamare tua madre?

Please, could you call your mom?

A che ora arrivi? Arriverò per le 5 del pomeriggio.

What time are you arriving? I will be there at about 5:00 p.m.

52. da/per – since/for

La mia famiglia conosce Pietro da molti anni. È un nostro amico.

My family has known Pietro for many years. He is a friend of ours.

Studio spagnolo da tre anni, ma ho ancora molto da imparare.

I have been studying Spanish for three years, but I still have a lot to learn.

Ho studiato francese per tre anni quando ero in Francia, ma ora ho dimenticato quasi tutto.

I studied French for three years when I was in France, but I have almost forgotten everything now.

53. caso – chance/case

Abbiamo conosciuto Sara per caso: eravamo alla fermata dell'autobus, il suo cellulare, è caduto e io l'ho raccolto.

We met Sara by chance: we were at the bus stop, her cell phone fell, and I picked it up.

Il caso del furto alla banca della città ha spaventato molte persone.

The bank robbery case scared many people.

54. conoscere/sapere – to know/to meet

Io e tuo padre ci conosciamo da molti anni. Ci siamo incontrati all'università.

Your father and I have known each other for many years now. We met at the university.

Tutti conoscono/sanno la verità, ma nessuno vuole parlare. Hanno tutti paura di te.

Everybody knows the truth, but nobody wants to speak. They are all scared of you.

Conosco molto bene questo libro, perché era il mio preferito quando ero piccola. L'ho letto molte volte, e conosco/so alcune parti a memoria.

I know this book very well, as it was my favorite one when I was a child. I have read it many times, and I know some parts by heart.

55. scuola – school

La scuola è una delle istituzioni più importante di uno stato, perché è dove si istruiscono le persone del futuro.

The school is one of the most important institutions of a state because it is where people of the future are educated.

Abbiamo scuole di pensiero diverse, ma possiamo trovare una soluzione al problema.

We have got two different schools of thought, but we can find a solution to the problem.

56. perdere – to lose

Ho fatto una dieta, e ho perso molti chili, ma devo ancora perderne alcuni.

I went on a diet, and I lost many kilos, but I have to lose some more.

Ieri la nonna ha parcheggiato la macchina nel garage del supermercato. Dopo aver fatto la spesa, non la trovava più! L'aveva persa.

Yesterday, my grandmother parked the car in the supermarket garage. After she did the shopping, she was not able to find it anymore! She had lost it.

Smettila di fare rumore! Sto perdendo la pazienza.

Stop making noises! I'm losing my patience.

57. allora – then/so/at the time

La segretaria ha ricevuto una chiamata da una collega di un altro ufficio, così ha avvertito il suo capo che non doveva andare alla riunione.

The secretary received a call from a colleague from another office, and she then informed her boss he did not have to attend the meeting.

Allora, come è andata la tua vacanza? Raccontami tutto!

So, how was your holiday? Tell me everything about it!

Quando mio nonno era piccolo, giocava per strada con i coetanei; allora, non c'erano molte macchine, e la strada era un posto più sicuro.

When my grandfather was a child, he used to play in the street with his mates; at the time, there were not many cars, and the street was a safer place.

58. poi – then

Ieri ho deciso di andare in spiaggia per pranzare col mio fidanzato. Abbiamo raggiunto un posto vicino al mare e poi ci siamo rilassati ascoltando il rumore delle onde. È stata una giornata magnifica!

Yesterday, I decided to go to the beach with my boyfriend for lunch. We reached a wonderful place near the sea, and then we relaxed, listening to the sound of the waves. It was a wonderful day!

59. far fare qualcosa a qualcuno – to make somebody doing something

Per la festa di Natale, la nostra maestra ci ha fatto fare dei biscotti, che poi abbiamo venduto.

For the Christmas party, our teacher had us make some cookies, which we then sold.

60. volare– to fly

In primavera, gli uccelli volano tra le nuvole, e fanno i loro nidi sui tetti.

During spring, birds fly among clouds, and they nest on roofs.

Quando prendiamo l'aereo per andare in Germania, voliamo sopra le Alpi; è uno spettacolo unico, soprattutto d'inverno, quando le montagne sono coperte di neve.

When we fly to Germany, we fly over the Alps; it is a unique sight, especially during winter, when mountains are covered by the snow.

61. vicino – near/close/neighbor

La chiesa vicino al mercato è molto antica. Fu costruita dai romani durante l'impero di Costantino, ed è uno degli edifici più belli della città.

The church near the market is very ancient. It was built by Romans during Constantine's empire, and it's one of the most beautiful buildings of the city.

Scusi, sa dov'è l'ufficio postale? Certamente, è proprio qui vicino.

Excuse me, do you know where the post office is? Sure, it's right here.

Il mio vicino è davvero fastidioso: ascolta sempre la musica a volume alto, corre, salta, e urla quando guarda le partite di calcio.

My neighbor is very annoying: he always listens to loud music, runs, jumps around the house, and screams when he watches soccer matches.

62. tempo – time/weather

Che tempo fa domani? Non lo so. Perché chiedi sempre a me com'è il tempo? Lo sai che non ascolto mai le previsioni metereologiche.

What's the weather like tomorrow? I do not know. Why do you always ask me what the weather is like? You know I do not ever listen to weather forecasts.

Ciao, Marisa! Quanto tempo! Come stai?

Hi, Marisa! Long time no see! How are you?

Il tempo passa per tutti, ma tu sei sempre la più bella.

Time passes by for everyone, but you are always the most beautiful.

63. sottolineare – to underline/to highlight

Quando studi, potresti provare a sottolineare le parti più importanti. Potrebbe aiutarti a memorizzare meglio ciò che devi imparare.

When you study, you could try to underline the most important parts. It could help you to better memorize what you have to learn.

Questa è un'occasione speciale, e vorrei sottolineare l'importanza di essere qui per tutti noi.

This is a very special occasion, and I would like to highlight the importance of being here for all of us.

64. ricordo – I remember/memory /souvenir

Mi ricordo quando andavo a scuola; anche se dovevo studiare molto, mi divertivo con i miei compagni di classe, sia dentro che fuori dall'aula.

I remember when I used to go to school: even if I had to study a lot, I had fun with my classmates, both inside and outside school.

Quando esco di casa non mi ricordo mai di chiudere la porta. È una cosa molto pericolosa perché potrebbero entrare i ladri.

When I leave home, I always forget to lock the door. It's a very dangerous thing because thieves could break in.

Pensando alla nostra infanzia, rievochiamo molti bei ricordi: i Natali in famiglia, giocare con i bambini, e tante risate.

Thinking about our childhood reminds us of so many good memories: Christmas with the family, playing with children, and lots of laughs.

I miei genitori sono andati in Thailandia a dicembre, e mi hanno portato tanti bei ricordini, tra cui conchiglie e oggetti di artigianato.

My parents went to Thailand in December, and they got me so many beautiful souvenirs, like shells and handicrafts.

65. il/lo – the

Il gatto sale sulla sedia, il topo si nasconde nel muro, e il cane li insegue.

The cat jumps on the chair, the mouse hides inside the wall, and the dog chases them.

Lo squalo è un animale meraviglioso, anche se molti pensano che sia pericoloso.

The shark is a wonderful animal, even if many people think it is dangerous.

Il cane è senza dubbio il migliore amico dell'uomo.

The dog is, no doubt, a man's best friend.

Lo studente deve scrivere il suo nome e il suo cognome su ogni foglio dell'esame.

The student has to write his/her name and his/her last name onto each exam paper.

66. i/gli – the

I gatti salgono sulle sedie, i topi si nascondono nel muro e i cani li inseguono.

Cats jump on the chairs, mice hide inside the wall, and dogs chase them.

Gli squali sono degli animali meravigliosi, anche se molti pensano che siano pericolosi.

Sharks are wonderful animals, even if many people think they are dangerous.

I cani sono senza dubbio i migliori amici degli uomini.

Dogs are, no doubt, men's best friends.

Gli studenti devono scrivere i loro nomi e i loro cognomi su ogni foglio dell'esame.

Students have to write their names and their last names onto each exam paper.

67. la/le – the

Il sole illumina il giorno, mentre la luna e le stelle illuminano la notte.

The sun brightens up the day, while the moon and the stars brighten up the night.

Giulia è l'amica di Lucia, ma anche Marta e Alessia sono sue amiche.

Giulia is Lucia's friend, but Marta and Alessia are her friends too.

Nell'alveare, c'è l'ape regina, e ci sono anche le api operaie.

In the beehive, there is the queen bee, and there are also worker bees.

68. un/uno – a/an

Uno spazio vuoto in una casa può essere riempito con un quadro.

An empty space in a house can be filled with a painting.

Un bambino camminava nel parco quando trovò un gioco. Lo mise vicino a un cespuglio, sperando che il proprietario lo ritrovasse.

A child was walking in the park when he found a toy. He put it next to a bush, hoping the owner could find it.

69. una/un' – a/an

Non c'è una soluzione a questo problema. Vi consiglio di comprare un altro computer.

There isn't a solution to this problem. I suggest you buy a new laptop.

Non tutti i momenti difficili portano qualcosa di positivo, ma rappresentano sicuramente un'opportunità di crescita.

Tough times do not always bring positive things, but they do represent an opportunity to grow up.

70. lungo/corto-breve – long/short

Per la festa di sabato sera, mia sorella ha scelto un abito lungo e nero, io invece uno corto e viola. Siamo completamente diverse.

For the Saturday night party, my sister chose a long black dress, while I chose a short purple one. We are completely different.

Per lungo tempo, gli uomini hanno cercato di controllare il mondo, e, quando ci sono riusciti, hanno iniziato a distruggerlo con l'inquinamento.

For a long time, humans tried to control the world, and when they succeeded, they started to destroy it with pollution.

Questa è la strada più corta/breve per arrivare alla chiesa. Fidati!

This is the shortest way to get to the church. Trust me!

71. alto/basso – tall-high/short

Quando si devono scattare le foto di gruppo, essere alti è utile perché non devi mai inginocchiarti. Se invece sei basso, devi sempre sederti.

When it comes to group shots, being tall is useful, as you do not ever need to kneel. Instead, if you are short, you always have to sit down.

L'alto numero di partecipanti al corso indica che le persone sono molto interessate, quindi dobbiamo fare del nostro meglio per non deluderle.

The high number of participants in the course indicates that people are very interested in it, so we must do our best not to disappoint them.

72. per davvero-veramente/attualmente – actually/at present/now

Non posso credere che tu l'abbia fatto. È stata una follia!

I can't believe you actually did it. That was insane!

Veramente, il mio nome completo è Maria Carmen Rossi, ma tutti mi chiamano Carmen da quando sono piccola. Non so esattamente perché.

Actually, my full name is Maria Carmen Rossi, but everybody has called me Carmen since I was a little girl. I do not know why.

Il ruolo che Luca attualmente ha nella compagnia è amministrativo più che gestionale. Infatti, non è felice, perché non gli piace molto.

Luca's company role is now more administrative than managerial. In fact, he is not happy, as he does not like it.

Attualmente, stiamo vivendo una situazione molto difficile a causa di diversi problemi familiari.

At the moment, we are experiencing a very hard situation due to many family problems.

73. infastidito/annoiato – annoyed/bored

È tutto il giorno che parli del tuo lavoro. Capisco che tu abbia dei problemi e che sia stressato, ma sono infastidita dal fatto che non mi hai chiesto niente sulla mia settimana.

You have been talking about your job all day long. I understand you are facing some problems and you are stressed, but I am very annoyed by the fact that you have not asked me anything at all about my week.

Alla cena di ieri sera, non c'era musica, e nessuno parlava. Eravamo tutti così annoiati che ci siamo messi a usare il cellulare.

At yesterday night's dinner, there was no music, and nobody was talking. We were all so bored that we started using our phones.

74. coraggioso/bravo in/bravo a – brave/good at

Sei una persona molto coraggiosa. Hai salvato quel bambino dall'incendio in pochi minuti.

You are very brave. You saved that child from the fire in no time.

Mio fratello è bravo in matematica, ma io sono più bravo di lui in letteratura.

My brother is good at math, but I am better than him at literature.

Sei bravo a giocare a tennis? Io sto imparando e mi piace molto.

Are you good at playing tennis? I am learning how to, and I'm really liking it.

75. macchina fotografia/camera – camera/room/bedroom

Le nuove macchine fotografiche digitali scattano delle foto bellissime, ma devi saperle usare. Non è facile.

The latest digital cameras take wonderful photos, but you have to know how to use them. It is not easy.

Questo hotel è il mio preferito: si trova in una posizione molto centrale, vicino alla spiaggia, e il servizio in camera è molto veloce. Ci veniamo ogni anno.

This is my favorite hotel: it's located in a central position, it's very close to the beach, and the room service is very fast. We come here every year.

La casa di Marco è molto grande: ha cinque stanze da letto, e la sua camera ha una finestra sul giardino.

Marco's house is very big: it has five bedrooms, and his room has a window on the garden.

76.
ragionevole/sensibile/sensitivo – sensible/sensitive/medium

Crescendo, si dovrebbe diventare più ragionevoli. Invece, spesso, è esattamente il contrario.

Growing up, we are supposed to become more sensible. However, it's often the other way round.

Mio nipote è un ragazzo molto sensibile: non è semplice per lui ricevere brutte notizie.

My nephew is a very sensitive boy: it is not easy for him to receive bad news.

La nonna di Cristina è una donna molto strana. Dice di essere una sensitiva, e per questo motivo, le persone vanno a casa sua sperando di parlare con i loro cari defunti.

Cristina's grandmother is a very weird woman: she says she is a medium, and for this reason, people go to her house, hoping to speak to their dearly departed ones.

77. fiducia/confidenza – confidence/familiarity

In un rapporto, la fiducia è la cosa più importante, perché se non c'è fiducia mancano le basi per il futuro.

In a relationship, trust is the most important thing, because if there is no trust, there is no ground for the future.

La famiglia Bianchi vive nel palazzo di fronte da più di vent'anni. Siamo molto amici e abbiamo confidenza; infatti, ci raccontiamo tutti i nostri segreti. Tutti sanno tutto di tutti.

The Bianchi family has been living in the front building for more than twenty years. We are good friends, and we are really close; in fact, we tell each other our secrets. Everybody knows everything about everyone.

78. esauriente/comprensivo – comprehensive/understanding/inclusive

La tua spiegazione sull'utilizzo dei nuovi dispositivi è stata esauriente. Credo che ora tutti abbiano i giusti strumenti per poter lavorare meglio e più velocemente.

Your explanation on how to use the new devices was very detailed. I believe that now everybody has the right tools that will allow them to work better and faster.

Non ce l'ho fatta a consegnare i compiti, ma il professore mi ha detto che ho ancora tempo e che posso consegnarli mercoledì. È stato molto comprensivo.

I didn't manage to hand in the homework on time, but the professor told me that I still have time and that I can hand them in on Wednesday. He was very understanding.

L'anno scorso abbiamo fatto una vacanza in Marocco e abbiamo alloggiato in un hotel meraviglioso. Abbiamo speso poco. Era tutto incluso, addirittura la SPA.

Last year, we took a vacation to Morocco in a wonderful hotel. We spent little money. It was all-inclusive, even the SPA.

79. marciapiede/pavimento – pavement/floor

In molte città italiane, i marciapiedi sono vecchissimi e strettissimi. A volte, sono così stretti da impedire il passaggio di due persone alla volta. È uno degli aspetti più caratteristici dell'Italia, ed è uno di quelli che amo di più, insieme alla cucina.

In many Italian cities, the pavements are very old and narrow. Sometimes, they are so narrow that two people can't walk on them at the same time. It is one of the most peculiar features of Italy, and one of those I love the most, together with food.

Dobbiamo cambiare il pavimento della nostra casa in campagna. L'allagamento lo ha rovinato. Ci costerà molto, e non avremo la casa pronta per la prossima estate. Che sfortuna!

We have to change our country house floor. A flood ruined it. It will cost us a lot, and the house won't be ready for the next summer. That's too bad!

80. comodo/conveniente – comfortable/convenient/cheap

Il nuovo divano di tua madre è troppo comodo! È così morbido. Le vorrei chiedere dove l'ha comprato così me lo compro anch'io.

The new couch your mother bought is very comfortable! It is so soft. I would like to ask her where she bought it so that I will buy it too.

Andare in treno a Venezia da Firenze è molto comodo. Ci sono le corse veloci, e i biglietti non costano molto.

Going by train from Florence to Venice is very convenient. There are fast trains, and the tickets are not very expensive.

Questa è la macchina più conveniente che il mercato offra, perché la puoi comprare in super sconto.

This is the cheapest car that the market offers, as you can get it with excellent promotions.

81. rivista/magazzino – magazine/warehouse

Nella mia famiglia leggiamo molte riviste. Mio padre ama le riviste di auto, mia madre quelle di cucina, e mio fratello solo riviste di computer. Per quanto riguarda me, io leggo sempre le riviste di moda.

In my family, we read many magazines. My father loves car magazines, my mother cooking magazines, and my brother only computer magazines. As for me, I always read fashion magazines.

Signora, devo andare in magazzino e controllare se ci sono le scarpe che desidera. Torno subito.

I have to go to the warehouse and check if there are the shoes you want, madame. I will be right back.

82. genitore/parente – parent/relative

I tuoi genitori sono davvero formidabili! Ti lasciano fare tutto quello che vuoi, e si fidano di te. I miei genitori invece sono molto rigidi, soprattutto mio padre, e non mi fanno mai uscire, neppure il sabato sera.

Your parents are really great! They let you do everything you want, and they trust you. Instead, my parents are very strict, especially my father, and they never let me go out, not even on a Saturday night.

Ci sono soltanto poche occasioni nelle quali è possibile riunire tutti i parenti insieme, e i matrimoni sono una di queste. Sono molto felice perché domenica ci sarà il matrimonio di mia cugina. Così potrò rivedere tanti parenti che non vedo da un bel po'.

There are only few occasions when you can gather all your relatives, and weddings are one of those. I am very happy because on Sunday there will be my cousin's wedding. I will be able to meet so many relatives that I have not seen for a while.

83. istruito/educato – educated/polite

Finire gli studi è molto importante perché essere istruito è un grande valore e ti dà maggiori opportunità lavorative.

Finishing your studies is very important because being educated is valuable and gives you more job opportunities.

Ieri ho incontrato un signore gentile. Stavo camminando quando la mia borsa è caduta, e tutto quello che c'era dentro si è sparso sul marciapiede. Lui mi ha aiutato a raccoglierlo. È stato così gentile da parte sua!

Yesterday, I met a nice man. I was walking when my bag fell, and everything inside was scattered on the ground. He helped me to pick everything up. It was so kind of him.

84. rendersi conto/realizzare – to realize/to carry out

I miei amici sono partiti per andare in campagna, lo scorso weekend. Stavano guidando da ore quando si sono resi conto di aver sbagliato strada. Ormai era tardi, e così sono tornati in città.

My friends left to go to the countryside last weekend. They had been driving for hours when they realized they took the wrong way. At that point, it was too late, and so they went back to the city.

Per realizzare questo lavoro, avrò bisogno di almeno una settimana. Se inizio questo non posso lavorare ad altri progetti.

To carry out this job, I will need at least one week. I can't work on other projects if I start this one.

85. alla fine/eventualmente – eventually/in case

Ieri è stato un giorno molto difficile e stancante. Prima siamo andati a fare la spesa e non abbiamo trovato parcheggio, allora abbiamo deciso di andare a cena fuori, ma non c'era posto in nessuno dei ristoranti che ci piacciono. Alla fine, siamo tornati a casa e abbiamo ordinato una pizza.

Yesterday it was a very hard and tiring day. First, we went shopping and did not find any parking, so we decided to go out for dinner, but all the restaurants we like were full. Eventually, we came back home and ordered a pizza.

Mi dispiace che la tua macchina si sia rotta. Eventualmente, se non la riparano entro venerdì, posso prestarti la mia per andare a Milano.

I'm sorry your car is broken. If they don't repair it before Friday, I can lend you mine to go to Milan.

86. romanzo/novella – novel/short story

Sono molti i romanzi famosi del diciannovesimo secolo, ma Delitto e Castigo di Dostoevskij è un capolavoro.

There are many famous novels from the nineteenth century, but Dostoevsky's *Crime and Punishment* is a masterpiece.

Uno dei metodi miglior per imparare una lingua è leggere le novelle. Infatti, è più facile leggere e capire una storia breve che un libro intero. Spesso le parole si ripetono, quindi non devi cercarle nel dizionario.

One of the best ways to learn a language is to read short stories. In fact, it is easy to read and understand a short tale than an entire book. Often, words are repeated, and so you do not have to look them up in the dictionary.

87. biblioteca/libreria – library/bookshop/bookcase

Ci sono studenti che amano studiare in biblioteca perché non hanno distrazioni e possono concentrarsi meglio. Altri invece preferiscono studiare a casa, dove hanno tutte le comodità di cui hanno bisogno.

There are students who love studying at the library because they do not have distractions and can concentrate better. Others, instead, prefer studying at home, where they have all the comforts they need.

Da quando gli e-book sono arrivati sul mercato, molte librerie, soprattutto quelle più piccole, hanno chiuso. Personalmente, preferisco il libro cartaceo, e amo andare in libreria perché posso scoprire sempre nuovi libri.

Since e-books arrived on the market, many bookshops, especially the smallest ones, closed. Personally, I prefer paper books, and I love going to the bookshop because I can always discover new ones.

Le librerie di design sono molto belle, ma alcune non possono ospitare molti libri. Le librerie delle case antiche sono più affascinanti perché sono piene di testi di ogni genere.

Designer bookcases are very beautiful, but some can't keep many books. Ancient houses' ones are more fascinating because they are full of all types of books.

88. ditta/firma – firm/signature

La maggior parte delle ditte italiane è famosa per produrre beni di alta qualità. Questo è sia ciò che le ha rese celebri in tutto il mondo, sia ciò che ha reso così importante il "Made" in Italy.

Most Italian firms are famous for producing high-quality goods. This is what has made them famous worldwide, and what has made the "Made" in Italy so important.

Questa mattina sono stata in banca per aprire un nuovo conto. Ho dovuto mettere così tante firme che alla fine, mi ha fatto male il polso.

This morning I went to the bank to open a new bank account. I had to put so many signatures that eventually, my wrist hurt.

89. piatto – dish/flat

Tutti i piatti nella dispensa erano di mia nonna. Non sono preziosi, ma mi piace usarli perché mi ricordano quando da piccola mi preparava il pranzo dopo la scuola.

All dishes in the pantry were my grandmother's. They are not valuable, but I like using them because they remind me of when I was a child, and she used to prepare me lunch after school.

La cucina thailandese è ottima. Include piatti molto saporiti ma anche molto leggeri.

Thai food is excellent. It includes both tasty and light dishes.

Gli antichi pensavano che la terra fosse piatta e che ci fosse un solo mare.

Ancient people believed that the Earth was flat and that there was only one sea.

90. dovere – duty/must/to have to

Il dovere di ogni cittadino è quello di comportarsi con educazione, rispettando la città e le altre persone che ci vivono.

Each citizen's duty is to behave politely, respecting the city and the others who live there.

Stasera c'è la festa a casa di Giovanni, e devo comprarmi un nuovo vestito. Vorrei tanto che mi notasse.

Tonight, it's Giovanni's party, and I must buy a new dress. I would love it if he noticed me.

Non dovete pagare la cena, perché è stata già pagata dall'azienda.

You don't have to pay for the dinner, because the company has already paid for it.

91. passato – past/passed

In passato, le persone vivevano con molti meno problemi rispetto a noi. Oggi siamo tutti stressati dal lavoro e dai nostri impegni quotidiani, al punto che ci dimentichiamo le cose belle che la vita potrebbe offrirci.

In the past, people lived with much less problems than we do. Nowadays, we are all stressed by work and by our daily tasks, to the point that we forget the beautiful things life can offer us.

Se stai cercando il supermercato, devi prendere la prima a destra, andare dritto e, passata la libreria, girare a sinistra. Lo troverai sulla tua destra, accanto alla banca.

If you are looking for the supermarket, you must take the first on the right, go straight, go past the bookshop and then turn left. You will find it on your right, next to the bank.

Per andare in Francia, siamo passati dalla Germania. Abbiamo guidato molto, ma è stato un giro interessante perché abbiamo visto dei paesini davvero graziosi.

To travel to France, we drove through Germany. We drove a lot. However, it was a very interesting tour, because we visited many pretty villages.

92. regalo – present/to give

La cosa più bella del Natale, da quando non sono più bambino, è la cena della vigilia del 24 e il pranzo di Natale del 25. Quando ero piccolo, non mi importava del cibo e pensavo solo ai regali.

The most beautiful thing about Christmas, since I am not a child anymore, is the Christmas Eve dinner on the 24th and the

Christmas lunch on the 25th. When I was younger, I did not care about food at all but thought only about presents.

Questo cappotto non mi va più bene, se vuoi te lo regalo.

This coat does not fit me anymore. If you want, I will give it to you.

93. accettare – to agree to/ to accept

Mi hanno proposto un lavoro a Roma e io ho accettato, nonostante Roma sia una città molto difficile in cui vivere. Sarà comunque un'esperienza positiva, e avrò l'opportunità di imparare molte cose.

I received a job proposal in Rome and accepted it, even though Rome is a very hard city to live in. Anyway, it will be a positive experience, and I will have the opportunity to learn a lot.

Non accettare mai offerte da sconosciuti. Non puoi sapere quali sono le loro intenzioni. È molto pericoloso.

Do not ever accept offers by strangers. You can't know their purposes. It is a very dangerous thing.

94. neve/nevicare – snow/ to snow

Quando dall'aereo vedo le montagne coperte di neve, provo una magnifica sensazione, e capisco la forza della natura.

When I see the mountains covered by the snow from the airplane, it is a wonderful feeling, and I understand the strength of nature.

Quest'inverno non ha nevicato molto, e la stagione sciistica è stata problematica. Molti alberghi hanno chiuso perché c'erano pochi clienti. Spero che il prossimo anno vada meglio.

This winter it didn't snow a lot, and the skiing season was problematic. Many hotels closed because there were few clients. I hope next year it will be better.

95. pioggia/piovere – rain/to rain

La pioggia ha molti effetti benefici per l'agricoltura, ma negli ultimi anni, con i livelli di inquinamento che abbiamo raggiunto, le piogge acide sono raddoppiate e hanno provocato molti danni.

The rain has many good effects for agriculture. But in the last years, with the pollution levels we reached, acid rains doubled and caused many damages.

La Gran Bretagna è famosa per molte cose, tra cui sicuramente il fatto che piova tanto e molto spesso. Non si può visitare Londra senza portarsi un ombrello appresso.

Great Britain is famous for many things, one of which is, for sure, the fact that it rains a lot and very often. It is impossible to visit London without taking an umbrella with you.

96. salato – salty/expensive

Il sugo ai funghi che hanno cucinato Marco e Susanna ieri sera era molto buono, solo che era troppo salato. Ho dovuto bere acqua tutta la notte.

The mushroom sauce Marco and Susanna cooked yesterday night was very good. The only problem was that it was too salty. I had to drink water all night long.

Siamo stati in un bellissimo ristorante sul lago. La vista era magnifica: si potevano vedere le montagne e le colline. La cena era ottima, solo che il conto si è rivelato molto salato rispetto a quello che abbiamo mangiato. Le porzioni erano molto piccole.

We went to a very beautiful restaurant on the lake. The view was wonderful: we could see the mountains and the hills. The dinner was excellent, but the bill was very expensive compared to what we ate. The portions were very small.

97. offendere – offend/to hurt somebody's feelings

Era lo scorso Natale. Sapevamo tutti che Pietro odiasse sua cognata, ma nessuno avrebbe potuto immaginare che la avrebbe offesa in quel modo. Si è alzato in piedi e ha iniziato a gridarle contro.

It was last Christmas. We all know that Pietro hates his mother-in-law, but nobody could imagine that he would have offended her in that way: he stood up and started yelling at her.

Non sono arrabbiata con te, ma sono molto triste per quello che mi hai fatto. Mi hai offesa, e non so se riuscirò mai a perdonarti.

I am not angry at you, but I am very sad because of what you did to me. You hurt my feelings, and I do not know if I will be able to forgive you anymore.

98. ci/ne – us/ourselves/to us/there/about something-someone/a certain quantity of something-someone

Non ci vediamo mai, ma sai che ti vogliamo bene e che faremmo qualsiasi cosa per te. Quindi, se hai problemi, chiamaci.

We never see each other, but you know that we love you and that we would do everything for you. So, if you have problems, call us.

Stavamo costruendo una barca di legno, e ci siamo tagliati tutti e due nello stesso momento. È stato un momento difficile ma anche divertente perché uno soccorreva l'altro senza successo.

We were building a wooden boat, and we both cut ourselves at the same time. It was difficult but also funny because we were helping each other without success.

I miei genitori ci hanno regalato due biglietti per il concerto di domani sera. Vorremo andarci ma abbiamo già un impegno. Li vuoi tu?

Our parents gave us two tickets for tomorrow night's concert. We would like to go, but we already have plans. Do you want them?

Gabriella mi ha raccontato del suo viaggio in Sicilia. Mi ha parlato di spiagge molto belle e di cibo buono ed economico. Ho deciso di andarci il prossimo anno.

Gabriella told me about her trip to Sicily. She told me about the beautiful beaches and the tasty and inexpensive food. I have decided to visit it next year.

Mia sorella era molto triste; aveva rotto con il suo ragazzo, ma non voleva parlarne. È rimasta nella sua camera a piangere per tre giorni.

My sister was very sad; she had broken up with her boyfriend, but she didn't want to talk about it. She cried in her room for three days.

Che belle mele! Me ne dà due chili per favore? Voglio fare una torta per mio marito. Stasera, è il suo compleanno.

Look at those apples! Could I get due kilos of them, please? I want to make a cake for my husband. Tonight, it is his birthday.

99. male – badly/rudely/evil things/evil

Quando dormi in un letto che non è il tuo, spesso dormi male, e il giorno dopo hai dolori in tutto il corpo. Questo succede anche quando dormi in un letto comodo.

When you sleep in a bed that is not yours, you often sleep badly, and the following day you have got pain all over your body. This also happens when you sleep in a good bed.

La scorsa, settimana sono andata nel negozio di abbigliamento al centro commerciale che mi avevi suggerito. Ho provato un po' di vestiti, ma quando ho chiesto alla commessa se avesse anche delle scarpe, lei mi ha risposto male dicendo che se volevo delle scarpe, sarei dovuta andare in un altro negozio. Me ne sono andata e non ho comprato nulla.

Last week, I went to the clothing store at the mall you suggested. I tried on many clothes, but when I asked the shop assistant if she had some shoes, she replied in a rude way, saying that, if I wanted shoes, I should have gone to another shop. I left without buying anything.

Sono felice che Mattia se ne sia andato: una persona del genere può solo farti del male.

I am happy Mattia left: a person like him can only do bad things to you.

Se pensiamo che la vita sia solo una lotta tra il bene e il male, ci sbagliamo.

If we think that life is only a battle of good against evil, we are wrong.

100. male – moreover/furthermore

Le conferenze dureranno tre giorni, e ogni ospite alloggerà nell'hotel. Inoltre, sono già stati consegnati loro i programmi delle giornate e i buoni pasto per le cene.

Conferences will last three days, and each guest will stay in the hotel. They have already been given the program and dinner meal tickets.

101.gamba – strenght/come on!

Ero così spaventato che mi tremavano le gambe. Non avevo mai visto un incidente automobilistico prima, e ho avuto molta paura. Per fortuna, nessuno si è ferito gravemente.

I was so scared that my legs were shaking. I had never seen a car accident before, and I was very frightened. Luckily, nobody was seriously injured.

Mi piace il nuovo stagista. È proprio un ragazzo in gamba; appena gli chiedi di fare qualcosa, lui coglie al volo la richiesta e lavora in fretta. Sicuramente, gli offriremo un contratto a fine apprendistato.

I like the new intern. He is a very capable guy; as soon as you ask him to do something, he understands and does the work very fast. We will offer him a contract at the end of the internship, for sure.

102. forza – strength/Come on!

Dopo gli allenamenti di calcio con la squadra, i ragazzi tornano a casa senza forze.

After soccer training with the team, the guys get home without strength.

Forza, andiamo! Il treno sta per partire, e dobbiamo ancora arrivare al binario. Se vogliamo prenderlo, dovremmo correre.

Come on, let's go! The train is about to leave, and we still have to get to the platform. If we want to take it, we will have to run.

103. io faccio/tu fai/lui fa – I; you do/ make/ she does/makes

Io di solito faccio la spesa la mattina presto, tu la fai la sera, e Marta non la fa mai.

I usually do the shopping early in the morning, you do it in the evening, and Marta never does it.

104. noi facciamo/loro fanno – we; they do/ make

Qualche volta facciamo i biscotti al cioccolato, ma i miei zii li fanno con la vaniglia.

Sometimes we make chocolate cookies, but my aunt and my uncle make vanilla ones.

105. fate – to do/make/ fairies

Voi non fate mai quello che vi dico; se volete superare il test, dovete ascoltarmi e studiare di più, con più concentrazione.

You never do what I tell you; if you want to pass the test, you will have to listen to me and study more and with more concentration.

Le bambine amano le storie delle principesse perché vengono sempre salvate da un principe bellissimo e aiutate dalle fate buone.

Little girls love princess stories because they are always saved by a handsome prince and helped by good fairies.

106. io so/tu sai/lei sa – I; you know/she knows

Hai affrontato molte difficoltà per arrivare a questi risultati, e so che non ti fermerai.

You have faced many difficulties to get to these results, and I know that you won't stop.

Sai dove sono le mie chiavi di casa? Non le trovo da nessuna parte.

Do you know where my house keys are? I can't find them anywhere.

Io non posso aiutarti, ma la mia amica Giulia sa la strada. Ora la chiamo.

I can't help you, but my friend Giulia knows the way. I will immediately call her.

107. noi sappiamo/voi sapete/loro sanno – we; you; they know

Noi sappiamo tutta la verità, e voi lo sapete, ma sapete anche che non la diremo a nessuno. Quindi, smettetela di preoccuparvi.

We know all the truth, and you know it, but you also know that we won't tell anybody. So, stop being worried.

Abbiamo già provato a chiedere a quelle persone al bar, ma loro non ne sanno niente. Sembra che nessuno abbia visto Marta da settimane.

We have already asked those people at the bar, but they do not know anything. It seems like nobody has seen Marta for weeks.

108. io bevo/tu bevi/lui beve – I; you drink/he drinks

Non faccio mai colazione. Bevo solo un caffè ed esco di casa.

I never have breakfast. I only drink a coffee and leave home.

Come mai non bevi il latte? È troppo caldo?

Why don't you drink your milk? Is it too hot?

Tommaso non beve mai quando guida. È un ragazzo serio.

Tommaso never drinks when he drives. He is a serious guy.

109. noi beviamo/voi bevete/loro bevono – we; you; they drink

Ogni domenica andiamo a cena da mia nonna. Beviamo sempre il vino rosso che produce il suo vicino.

Every Sunday, we go to my grandmother's house for dinner. We always drink the red wine her neighbor makes.

Non saprete mai quanto è buono questo succo fino a che non lo berrete.

You will never know how good this juice is until you drink it.

I ragazzi di oggi bevono molto, ma non fa bene alla salute.

These days, guys drink a lot, but it's not healthy.

110. io mi siedo/tu ti siedi/lei si siede– I; you sit down/she sits down

Scusatemi, ma non posso continuare a camminare. Mi siedo qui e riposo un po'.

Sorry, but I can't keep walking. I will sit here and rest for a while.

Perché quando prendi il treno ti siedi sempre dal lato del finestrino?

Why do you always sit next to the window when you take the train?

Paolo è un mio compagno di classe. Non lo sopporto, ma lui tutte le mattine si siede vicino a me.

Paolo is one of my classmates. I can't stand him, but he sits next to me every morning.

111. noi ci sediamo/voi vi sedete/loro si siedono – we; you; they sit down

Quando andate al cinema, vi sedete sempre in prima fila, mentre noi ci sediamo sempre al centro. Non potremmo mai andarci insieme.

When you go to the cinema, you always sit in the front row, and we always sit in the middle instead. We could not ever go to the cinema together.

Dopo il lavoro, molti impiegati si siedono al parco, soprattutto durante l'estate.

After work, many employees sit in the park, especially during the summer.

112. io sto/tu stai/lui sta– I; you stay/he stays

Voi andate a cercarla dentro al centro commerciale. Io sto qui così se torna trova qualcuno.

Go look for her inside the mall. I will stay here so that if she comes back, she will find somebody.

Stai qui, per favore. Ho paura.

Stay here, please. I am scared.

Quando Sergio viene in città non sta mai dai suoi genitori, ma va sempre dal suo amico Carlo.

When Sergio comes to the city, he never stays at his parents' house, but always goes to his friend, Carlo.

113. noi stiamo/voi state/loro stanno – we; you; they stay

Durante l'inverno, la domenica non usciamo mai. Stiamo in casa a leggere o guardare film alla TV.

During winter, we never go out on Sundays. We stay home reading or watching a movie on TV.

Ragazzi, fate attenzione! Non state mai dove non possa vedervi.

Guys, be careful! Do not stay where I can't see you.

Ogni volta che fanno qualcosa di sbagliato, stanno a scuola un'ora in più.

Every time they do something wrong, they stay at school one extra hour.

114. io scelgo/tu scegli/lei sceglie– I; you choose/she chooses

Sono tutti dei vestiti molto belli, ma io scelgo questo verde. Tu quale scegli?

They are all beautiful dresses, but I will choose the green one. Which one are you going to choose?

Marina è molto sfortunata con i fidanzati: sceglie sempre quello sbagliato.

Marina is very unlucky with her boyfriends: she always chooses the wrong one.

115. noi scegliamo/voi scegliete/loro scelgono– we; you; they choose

Questi piatti sono tutti ottimi. Noi scegliamo il manzo, voi che cosa scegliete?

These dishes are all excellent. We will choose the meat, what are you going to choose?

Io proprio non li capisco. Non scelgono mai la via più semplice per risolvere i loro problemi.

I can't really understand them. They never choose the easiest way to solve their problems.

116. io vengo/tu vieni/lui viene– I; you come/he comes

Non credo che arriveremo tutti allo stesso orario; io vengo in macchina, tu vieni in moto, e Simone viene in treno. Troviamoci direttamente alla festa, è la cosa migliore.

I do not think we will all arrive at the same time. I'm coming by car, you are coming by motorbike, and Simone by train. We will meet directly at the party. It is the best thing.

117. noi veniamo/voi venite/loro vengono– we; you; they come

Ti piace questo bar? Ci veniamo tutte le mattine a fare colazione. Hanno molti tipi di cornetti e i proprietari sono molto simpatici. Anche Marco e Sara ci vengono spesso.

Do you like this bar? We come here every morning to have breakfast. They have many types of croissants, and the owners are very nice. Marco and Sara often come here too.

Se venite con noi, vi mostreremo uno dei posti più rilassanti del mondo.

If you come with us, we will show you one of the most relaxing places of the world.

118. io vado/tu vai/lei va– I; you go/she goes

Tuo fratello non va quasi mai a cena da vostra madre, e tu invece ci vai quasi tutti i giorni. Come mai? Hanno litigato?

Your brother hardly ever goes to dinner at your mother's house, but you go there almost every day. Why? Did they fight?

Non mi piace andare a teatro. Quando ci vado, è solo perché mia madre mi costringe.

I do not like going to the theater. If I go, it is only because my mother forces me.

119. noi andiamo/voi andate/loro vanno – we; you; they go

Dividiamoci! Voi andate da quella parte e noi andiamo da questa. Ci incontreremo qui tra un'ora.

Let's split up! You will go to that side, and we will go on this side. We will meet here in one hour.

Sono persone molto riservate. Vanno da soli ovunque e non amano i luoghi affollati.

They are very discreet people. They go alone everywhere and do not love crowded places.

120. io salgo/tu sali – I; you go up

Non uso mai l'ascensore, perché salgo sempre a piedi. Mi fa bene alla salute.

I never use the elevator, because I always take the stairs. It is good for my health.

Appena sali sul tetto, troverai il pallone che i ragazzi hanno lanciato.

As soon as you get to the roof, you will find the ball the guys threw.

121. voi salite/loro salgono – you; they go up

Siete una famiglia un po' strana. Voi salite sempre in macchina davanti a casa, ma vostra madre e vostra sorella salgono dopo un isolato.

You are a weird family. You always get into the car in front of your house, but your mother and sister get in after one block.

122. noi saliamo – we go up/ we salt

Saliamo sulla montagna per trovare la pace, non per allenarci.

We climb the mountain to find peace, not to train.

Ma quanto sale stai usando per la carne? Noi in casa saliamo poco.

How much salt are using for the meat? At home, we add very little salt.

123. sale– she/he goes out/salt

Il mio gatto sale sempre sulle sedie e, da lì, sul tavolo. Non posso mai lasciare la porta aperta quando sopra c'è del cibo; altrimenti, ci sale sopra e mangia tutto quello che trova.

My cat always jumps on the chairs and, from there, to the table. I can never leave the door open when there is food on the table; otherwise, my cat would get on it and eat everything he finds.

Per condire l'insalata non possono mancare olio, sale, e succo di limone.

To season the salad, we need oil, salt, and lemon juice.

124. io dico/tu dici/lui dice – I; you say/tell/he says/tells

Non devi dirmi quello che devo dire. Io dico quello che voglio.

You do not have to tell me what to say. I say what I want.

La maestra dice che Carlo è un bambino molto intelligente, ma che non si impegna molto.

The teacher says that Carlo is a very clever child, but that he does not work enough.

125. noi diciamo/voi dite/loro dicono – we; you; they say/tell

Voi dite che loro hanno rotto il vaso, loro dicono che lo avete rotto voi; chi dice la verità?

You say that they broke the pot, and they say you broke it; who is telling the truth?

Uno dei nostri difetti più grandi è che non diciamo mai quello che pensiamo apertamente, ma cerchiamo sempre di dire quello che le persone vorrebbero sentire.

One of our greatest flaws is that we never say openly what we are thinking, but we always try to say what people would like to hear.

126. io esco/tu esci/lei esce – I; you go out/she goes out

Mi piace andare al lavoro in bici. Se esco e sta piovendo, a volte prendo la macchina, e delle altre vado in bicicletta con l'ombrello.

I like going to work by bicycle. If I go out and it is raining, I sometimes take the car, and sometimes take the umbrella and go by bicycle.

A che ora esci da scuola il sabato? Non vado a scuola il sabato, ma esco con i miei amici.

What time does your school finish on Saturday? I do not go to school on Saturday; I go out with my friends instead.

Sara ha la mia stessa età, ma esce tutte le sere. Io posso uscire solo il sabato.

Sara is my same age, but she goes out every night. I can only go out on Saturday.

127. noi usciamo/loro escono – we; they go out

Usciamo da questa stanza perché puzza di broccoli, e noi li odiamo. Torneremo quando aprirete le finestre.

We are leaving this room because it smells like broccoli, which we hate. When you open the windows, we will come back.

I miei vicini di casa sono molto abitudinari: di mattina, escono sempre alla stessa ora, e di sera tornano sempre a casa alle otto.

Our neighbors are very methodical: they always go out at the same time in the morning and come back home always at 8:00 p.m.

128. uscite – you go out/exits

Non capisco perché quando uscite per andare al lavoro non prendiate la macchina invece dell'autobus, che ci mette molto più tempo.

I do not understand why, when you go out to go to work, you never take the car instead of the bus, which takes much more time.

In questo aereo, le uscite di sicurezza si trovano al centro e nella parte anteriore.

In this aircraft, emergency exits are in the middle and in the front part.

129. prova – test/proof/competition/attempt/rehearsal

L'esame di lingua ha tre prove: la parte scritta, quella di ascolto, e la prova orale, che è la più semplice.

The language exam has three tests: the written part, the listening one, and the oral test, which is the easiest one.

Il sospettato ha fornito la prova della sua innocenza. Aveva un alibi: infatti, tutti hanno confermato che la sera del delitto, si trovava nel pub sotto casa.

The suspect gave proof of his innocence. He had an alibi: in fact, everybody confirmed that the night of the crime, he was in the pub near his house.

La gara di domani è divisa in due parti: una ciclistica e una di nuoto.

Tomorrow's competition is divided into two parts: a cycling and a swimming one.

Questa è solo una prova. Domani cercheremo di capire se il nuovo sistema funziona davvero.

This is only an attempt. Tomorrow, we will try to understand if the new system really works.

Carla stasera non può venire con noi; ha la prova in teatro per lo spettacolo che sta preparando con la scuola, e lei è la protagonista.

Carla can't come with us tonight: she has the theater rehearsal for the show she is preparing with the school. She is the main character.

130. questo/questa/quest'– this

Questo è l'ultimo passaggio; ora inforniamo la torta.

This is the last step. Now, let's bake the cake.

Non aprire questo cassetto, ci sono i miei documenti personali.

Do not open this drawer; there are my personal files in there.

Abbiamo preso questa decisione per il bene della comunità.

We have made this decision for the community's sake.

Quest'inverno sarà molto freddo.

This winter will be very cold.

Non credo che quest'espressione possa essere usata in questo contesto.

I do not think this expression can be used in this context.

131. questi/queste – these

State attenti! Questi scalini sono pericolosi.

Watch out! These steps are dangerous.

Questi amici sono spagnoli. Vengono da Madrid.

These friends are Spanish. They come from Madrid.

Non scrivete su queste cartoline, useremo queste qui che sono nuove.

Do not write on these postcards. We will use these new ones.

Queste accuse non hanno una logica, non sono fondate.

These accusations do not follow a logic. They are baseless.

132. quel/quello/quella/quell' – that

Quel bambino laggiù è il fratello di Andrea; è un ottimo giocatore di tennis e ha un grande futuro.

That child over there is Andrea's brother. He is an excellent tennis player and has a great future ahead.

Quello non è uno squalo; non preoccupatevi! È solo un tonno.

It is not a shark; do not worry! It is only a tuna.

La commissione ha deciso che quella fosse l'unica soluzione per questo problema.

The commission decided that was the only solution to this problem.

Quando eravamo piccoli, ci piaceva molto arrampicarci su quell'albero laggiù, dove ci sono quelle rocce.

When we were younger, we liked climbing that tree over there, where those rocks are.

Quell'abitudine che avevi di non toglierti le scarpe prima di entrare era pessima. Sono felice che tu abbia imparato a farlo.

That habit of yours of not taking your shoes off before getting inside was the worst. I am happy you learned to do it.

133. quei/quegli/quelle – those

Quei bambini in piazza devono stare molto attenti perché non è un'area pedonale. Ci passano le macchine.

Those children in the square must be very careful because it is not a pedestrian area. Cars drive there.

Andate sempre dritti. La mensa è di fronte alla biblioteca, là dove ci sono quegli studenti in fila.

Go always straight. The canteen is in front of the library, where there are those students standing in the line.

Quegli edifici in fondo alla strada sono stati tutti costruiti dopo la seconda guerra mondiale.

Those buildings at the end of the street were all built after World War II.

Vorrei un po' di quelle arance. Quanto costano?

I would like some of those oranges. How much are they?

Non ci sono problemi, potete sedervi dove volete perché tutte quelle sedie sono tutte libere.

No problem: you can sit where you want, as all of those chairs are available.

134. sùbito/subìto (consider that you will not find the accent generally, it is only to make you understand the different pronunciation) – right away/immediately/suffered/undergone

Vieni sùbito qui! Non voglio ripetertelo un'altra volta.

Come here right away! I won't tell you once again.

Mi scusi, potrei avere un'altra forchetta? La mia è caduta per terra. Certo signorina, gliene porto sùbito un'altra.

Excuse me, could I have another fork? Mine has fallen on the floor. Sure, miss, I will immediately get you another one.

Non è l'unico bambino che abbia subìto delle ingiustizie. Tutti noi abbiamo il dovere di fare di più per tutti quei bambini poveri.

He is not the only child in the world that has suffered injustices. Every one of us has the duty to make more for all those poor children.

Lo spettacolo non è andato molto bene, e il regista ha subìto molte critiche.

The show didn't go too well, and the director underwent many critiques.

135. prìncipi/princìpi (consider that you will not find the accent generally, it is only to make you understand the different pronunciation) – princes/beginning/origin/fundamentals/principles

In tutte le fiabe per bambini, i prìncipi cavalcano sempre un cavallo bianco.

In all fairy tales for kids, princes always ride a white horse.

Ai princìpi, qui non c'era nulla; ora ci sono case, bar, negozi, e ristoranti. È tutto molto cambiato negli ultimi vent'anni.

At the beginning, there was nothing here; now there are houses, bars, shops, and restaurants. Everything has changed a lot during these last twenty years.

Stefano perse il lavoro, e venne licenziato, mentre Carla aveva smesso di amarlo. Quello fu il principio della fine del loro rapporto.

Stefano lost his job, and he got fired while Carla did not love him anymore. That was the origin of the end of their relationship.

Buongiorno a tutti! Oggi parleremo di uno dei più importanti principi della fisica.

Good morning, everyone! Today we are speaking about one of the most important fundamentals of physics.

Mia nonna era una persona molto fredda, ma mi ha insegnato dei principi di vita che mi aiutano oggi, che mi hanno aiutato a crescere in passato, e che mi aiuteranno in futuro.

My grandmother was very aloof, but she taught me some life principles that still help me today, that helped me to grow up in the past, and that will help me in the future.

136. pesca (with a closed sound of the "e")/pesca (with an open sound of the "e" like lui è [he is])/ – fishing/peach

Sembra che la pesca sia uno degli hobby preferiti tra i pensionati, ma non credo che andrò a pesca quando smetterò di lavorare.

It looks like fishing is among retirees' favorite hobbies, but I do not think I will go fishing when I retire.

La pesca è uno dei miei frutti preferiti. In estate, ne mangio tante.

The peach is one of my favorite fruits. In summer, I eat a lot of them.

137. freddo/caldo – cold/hot/warm

Il tè freddo ha un sapore completamente diverso da quello caldo. Io lo bevo solo freddo, e mio marito solo caldo.

Iced tea has a completely different taste from the hot one. I only drink cold tea, and my husband only hot tea.

Il caldo sarà insopportabile. Andiamo in campagna.

The heat will be unbearable. Let's go to the countryside.

In molti pensano che il freddo sia peggiore del caldo, ma probabilmente non hanno mai provato a passare una giornata intera nel deserto.

Many people think that the cold weather is worse than the hot, but they have probably never spent a whole day in the desert.

La primavera è una stagione molto bella, ma anche molto strana: di giorno, fa caldo, e la sera, invece fa fresco. È molto facile ammalarsi.

Spring is a very beautiful season, but it's also a weird one: during the day, it is warm, and in the evening, it gets cold. It is very easy to get sick.

138. che/il quale/la quale/i quali/le quali – who/whom/that/which

I ragazzi che/i quali ho appena salutato, sono tutti miei compagni di classe. Sono molto simpatici, dovresti conoscerli.

The boys that I just greeted are all classmates of mine, and they are all very nice. You should meet them.

Tutte le persone che/le quali vorranno partecipare al concorso dovranno iscriversi entro i termini.

All the people that will want to take part in the competition will have to register within the deadlines.

In questo giardino ci sono tutti i cani che/i quali sono stati abbandonati. Se non trovano una casa, li portiamo al canile e aspettiamo una famiglia che/la quale li voglia adottare.

In this garden, there are all the dogs that were abandoned. If they do not find a home, we will take them to the shelter and wait for a family that wants to adopt them.

Tutte le opzioni che/le quali vi abbiamo offerto sono ancora valide. Avete tempo per scegliere.

All the options we offered are still valid. You have time to choose.

139. di cui/del quale/della quale/dei quali/delle quali – whose/of which/about which

Hai avuto un comportamento di cui/del quale dovresti solo vergognarti. È un argomento di cui abbiamo parlato molte volte. Se la scuola mi richiamerà, non giocherai per un mese ai videogiochi.

You should be ashamed of your behavior. It is a matter we talked about many times. If the school calls me back once again, you won't play videogames for a month.

140. per cui/per il quale/per la quale/per i quali/per le quali – so/which is why/for which

I voli durante le vacanze di Natale costavano molto, per cui ho deciso di aspettare febbraio per pagare molto meno.

During the Christmas holidays, flights were very expensive. So, I decided to wait for February and pay much less.

Erano molto stanchi dopo il viaggio, per cui sono andati direttamente in hotel. Spero di vederli domani sera.

They were very tired after the trip, which is why they went straight to the hotel. I hope to see them tomorrow night.

Questa sarebbe la donna per cui soffri dallo scorso anno? Immagino che abbia qualcosa di molto speciale.

This is the woman you have been suffering for since last year? I suppose she must be very special.

141. uomo/donna/ uomini/donne – man/ woman/men/women/ human being

Uomini e donne hanno abitudini e capacità diverse, ma entrambi possono fare le stesse cose, gli stessi lavori, e occuparsi della casa e della famiglia.

Men and women have different habits and skills, but they can both do the same things, the same jobs, and take care of the house and the family.

Le donne dell'età vittoriana amavano curare la casa, e usavano stoffe pregiate e oggetti decorativi molto belli.

Victorian-age women loved taking care of their house: they used fine fabrics and very beautiful decorative objects.

Oggigiorno, gli uomini curano il loro aspetto tanto quanto le donne.

Nowadays, men take care of their appearance as much as women do.

Il surriscaldamento globale dovuto all'inquinamento è causato dalle azioni inconsapevoli degli uomini.

Global warming, resulting from pollution, is caused by the unaware actions of human beings.

142. data/dato – date/data/given/fact/certain

Mio padre non si ricorda mai la data dell'anniversario di matrimonio, e ogni anno mia madre si arrabbia con lui.

My father never remembers his wedding anniversary date, and every year my mother gets mad at him.

I dati informatici della nostra azienda sono protetti da un sistema di sicurezza.

The computer data of our company are protected by a security system.

Perché non mi hai dato il tuo cellulare per fare quella chiamata? Scusami, è scarico.

Why didn't you lend me your cell phone to make that call? Sorry, the battery ran out.

Un dato molto importante per il nostro sondaggio è l'età delle persone.

An important fact for our survey is the age of people.

Modificando un dato elemento, si ottiene una nuova reazione chimica.

By modifying a certain element, we obtain a new chemical reaction.

143. saltare/salpare – to jump/to fail/ to go out/ to skip/to set sail

Il barboncino è un cane molto agile; salta incredibilmente in alto per la sua taglia ed è anche capace di fare le piroette sulle zampe posteriori.

The poodle is a very agile dog: it jumps incredibly high for its size and is also able to spin on its hind legs.

L'accordo è saltato per un piccolo dettaglio. Speriamo di poterlo concludere al più presto.

The agreement is skipped due to a small detail. We hope to close it as soon as possible.

A causa del temporale, la luce è saltata in tutto il quartiere.

Due to the storm, the energy went out in the entire neighborhood.

Potresti rileggere da capo? Credo che tu abbia saltato un passaggio molto interessante.

Could you please reread it from the beginning? I think you skipped a very interesting section.

Il Titanic salpò il 10 aprile, 1912 per il suo primo e ultimo viaggio verso New York.

Titanic set sail on April 10, 1912, for its first and last trip to New York.

144. pasto/pasta/paste – meal/pasta/dough/temperament /pastry

La mensa sarà aperta solo per l'orario dei pasti. Durante il resto della giornata, sarà possibile acquistare acqua, caffè, e altre bevande presso il bar collocato al piano terra.

The canteen will be open only at mealtimes. During the rest of the day, it will be possible to purchase water, coffee, and other drinks at the bar located on the ground floor.

La pasta è, come tutti sappiamo, il cibo italiano per eccellenza. Ne esistono di vari tipi, ma più famoso è lo spaghetto.

As we all know, pasta is the most important Italian food. There are many types of pasta, but the most famous one is spaghetti.

Quando mia nonna faceva la pasta per la pizza, la metteva nel forno a lievitare.

When my grandmother used to make the dough for the pizza, she would put it inside the oven to make it rise.

Quel ragazzo è di buona pasta: non si lamenta mai ed è sempre disponibile, e gentile con tutti.

That guy has a very good temperament: he never complains, and he is always willing and kind to everyone.

Tutti i bar italiani vendono cornetti, bomboloni, e zeppole (una pasta tipica). Gli italiani, infatti, fanno colazione con caffè o cappuccino e una pasta.

Every Italian bar sells croissants, puffs, and zeppole (a typical pastry). In fact, Italians have breakfast with a coffee or a cappuccino and a pastry.

145. giocare/giovare – to play/to improve/to benefit from

Giocare è molto importante perché dà l'opportunità di allenare il cervello, e può giovare alla memoria.

Playing is very important because it's an opportunity to train the brain, and it can improve memory.

Se completi gli studi, ne potrai giovare in futuro.

If you complete your studies, you will benefit from it in the future.

146. testo/testa/teste – text/I test/head/lead/witness

Scrivere un testo può sembrare semplice, ma in realtà non lo è. Bisogna fare attenzione alla struttura, ai contenuti e costruire frasi che abbiano una logica e siano corrette.

Writing a text can look easy, but in reality, it is not. You need to pay attention to the structure and the contents and build sentences that follow a logic and are correct.

Sono molto felice, perché questa notte finalmente, testerò il mio nuovo materasso. Erano anni che dormivo male.

I am very happy because tonight finally, I will test my new mattress. I slept badly for years.

La testa si trova sul collo. È la parte superiore del corpo.

The head is on the neck. It is the upper part of the body.

Il pilota si trovava in testa quando la sua auto si è guastata, e lui ha dovuto abbandonare la gara.

The pilot was in the lead when his car broke down, and he had to drop out of the race.

Il teste non ha nient'altro da aggiungere a quello che ha già detto.

The witness has nothing to add to what he has already said.

147. onore/onere – reputation/honor/privilege/duty

Dopo l'umiliazione subita, giurarono di vendicare il loro onore.

After the humiliation they had suffered, they swore to revenge their reputation.

Vostro onore, il caso è infondato.

Your Honor, the case is baseless.

Signori e signore, è con grande onore che vi presento la protagonista della serata.

Ladies and gentlemen, it is a great privilege to introduce you to tonight's protagonist.

Portare i turisti sulla cima della montagna è un grande onere. Non so se lo farò.

Taking tourists to the top of the mountain is a big duty. I do not know if I will do it.

148. guardare/guadare – to look at/to watch/ to check/ to ford

Guarda le stelle in cielo! Questa notte sono tante e sono molto luminose. Forse puoi esprimere un desiderio.

Look at the stars in the sky! There are a lot of them tonight, and they are very bright. Maybe you can make a wish.

Guardare troppa TV non fa bene agli occhi.

Watching too much TV is not good for your eyes.

Mamma, non trovo le mie scarpe nuove, sai dove possono essere? Guarda nella tua stanza.

Mom, I can't find my new shoes. Do you know where they might be? Check your bedroom.

Abbiamo fatto una vacanza in Costa Rica. Le spiagge erano bellissime, e le persone molto simpatiche. Ma la cosa più divertente ed eccitante è stata guadare i fiumi con il fuoristrada.

We took a holiday to Costa Rica. Beaches were beautiful, and people were very nice, but the funniest and most exciting thing was to ford rivers with the jeep.

149. supportare/sopportare – to prop up/to support/to bear/to stand

Abbiamo installato un programma che non era supportato dal nostro sistema operativo e quindi non funzionava.

We installed a program that was not supported by our operating system. That's why it did not work.

Dopo aver traslocato nella casa nuova, abbiamo messo tutti i libri su una mensola. La mensola non ha sopportato il peso ed è caduta.

After we had moved to the new house, we put all the books on a shelf, which did not prop the weight up and fell down.

Maria ed io siamo amiche da molti anni. Abbiamo condiviso gioie e dolori, ma, soprattutto, ci siamo supportate a vicenda nei momenti difficili.

Maria and I have been friends for many years. We have shared joys and sorrows, but, above all, we have supported each other through difficult moments.

Questa è l'ultima volta. Non sopporterò mai più una situazione così.

This is the last time. I won't bear a situation like this anymore.

Michele non lo sopporto. Vuole sempre stare al centro dell'attenzione ed è molto egoista.

I can't stand Michele. He always wants to grab all the attention. He is so selfish.

150. decidere/decedere – to decide/to decease

Non è stato facile decidere, ma poi abbiamo scelto la macchina rossa. Era più economica.

It was not an easy decision, but we chose the red car. It was the cheapest.

Sfortunatamente, mio zio è deceduto l'anno scorso. Aveva una patologia cardiaca.

Unfortunately, my uncle passed away last year. He had a heart disease.

151. volta – time/vault

Non te lo dirò un'altra volta: lasciami in pace.

I won't repeat it another time: leave me alone.

I latini dicevano che ripetere era d'aiuto. Glielo abbiamo detto una volta questa settimana, due volte la scorsa, e almeno tre volte quella ancora prima. Non vogliono ancora capirlo.

Latins used to say that repeating was helpful. We told them once this week, twice last week, and three times the week before the last one. They still do not want to understand it.

Nei battisteri romanici, venivano utilizzate volte a crociera perché lasciavano entrare più luce.

In Romanic baptisteries, they used ribbed vaults as they let more light in.

152. amante – lover/enthusiast/loving

L'opinione pubblica ha criticato la notizia dei due amanti fuggiti insieme dopo aver lasciato le proprie famiglie.

Public opinion criticized the news concerning two lovers who escaped together after having left their own families.

Mio padre è un vero amante del vino rosso di Toscana. Ogni anno, nel periodo della vendemmia, va in Toscana, e assaggia i vini delle più importanti cantine della regione.

My father is a true Tuscany red wine enthusiast. Every year, during the harvest season, he goes to Tuscany, and he tastes the wines of the most important producers of the region.

L'amante, dopo che la sua ragazza se ne andò, pianse giorno e notte.

The lover, after his girlfriend left, cried night and day.

153. chi – who

Scusami, chi sei? Il tuo viso mi sembra familiare.

Sorry, who are you? Your face looks familiar.

Con chi siete andati al cinema ieri?

Who did you go to the cinema with yesterday?

154. how – come

Come possiamo arrivare alla stazione senza prendere i mezzi di trasporto?

How can we get to the station without taking any means of transport?

Come stanno i tuoi genitori? L'ultima volta che li ho visti eravamo al mare. Era lo scorso anno.

How are your parents doing? Last time I saw them, we were at the beach. It was last year.

Come si chiama il tuo cane?

What is your dog's name?

155. dove – where

Dove siete? Noi siamo già arrivati, ma non vi vediamo.

Where are you? We have already arrived, but we can't see you.

Da dove viene la tua amica? Viene dalla Cina, ma è nata e cresciuta negli Stati Uniti. Si è trasferita in Cina quando aveva quindici anni.

Where does your friend come from? She comes from China, but she was born and grew up in the United States. She moved to China when she was fifteen years old.

156. quando - when

Quando avete deciso di cambiare auto?

When did you decide to change your car?

Da quanto tempo mi stai aspettando? Scusami, non volevo arrivare in ritardo ma c'era molto traffico.

How long have you been waiting for me? Sorry, I did not want to be late, but there was a lot of traffic.

157. perché – why/because

Perché non ci hanno portato quello che avevamo chiesto? Perché hanno detto che non era più disponibile. Dovremo scegliere qualcos'altro.

Why haven't they brought us what we had asked for? Because it was not available anymore, they said. We will have to choose something else.

158. che cosa – what

Mi potresti dire che cosa c'è che non va? Sono qui per aiutarti.

Could you tell me what is wrong? I am here to help you.

Per che cosa siamo venuti se non c'è nessuno che ci aspetti?

What have we come here for if there is nobody waiting for us?

159. quale – what/which

Ma che bella bambina! Quale nome sceglierete?

What a beautiful girl! What name will you choose?

Ci sono due sentieri che ci porterebbero alla chiesa sulla collina. Quale prendiamo? Il più facile, ovviamente.

There are two paths that could take us to the church upon the hill. Which one will we take? The easiest one, of course.

160. quanto/quanta – how much

Quanto ci vuole per arrivare a casa tua, da qui? Circa un'ora di macchina.

How long does it take to get to your house from here? About one hour by car.

Quanta pasta devo cuocere per quattro persone, considerando che Paolo mangia molto?

How much pasta do I have to cook for four people, considering that Paolo eats a lot?

161. quanti/quante – how many

Quanti fratelli hai? Nessuno, sono figlio unico.

How many brothers or sisters have you got? No one, I am an only child.

Quanti anni hanno le tue amiche? Sembrano più piccole di te.

How old are your friends? They look younger than you.

Quante volte ti ho detto che era pericoloso saltare da quel muretto?

How many times have I told you that jumping off that ledge was dangerous?

162. esatto – correct/right

Mi dispiace, ma il numero digitato non è esatto. Si prega di riprovare.

I am sorry, but the number you dialed is wrong. Please, try again.

Qual è l'organizzazione per domani? Ci vediamo davanti all'albergo alle 9 esatte. Non fare tardi.

What plans do we have for tomorrow? We are meeting in front of the hotel at 9 o'clock. Do not be late.

Esatto! Questa è la risposta corretta. Congratulazioni, ha vinto il primo premio.

Correct! This is the right answer. Congratulations, you have won the first prize.

163. falso/sbagliato – false/lie/fake/wrong

La risposta numero dieci era falsa. Forse è l'unica che ho sbagliato nel quiz.

Answer number ten was false. Maybe it's the only one I got wrong in the quiz.

Dire il falso non è mai una scelta intelligente, specie se si ha a che fare con una questione legale.

Telling a lie is never a smart choice, especially if you are dealing with a legal matter.

Le marche prestigiose hanno molti falsi. Acquistarli è reato, tanto quanto produrli e venderli.

There are many prestigious brands fakes. Purchasing them is a crime, as much as producing and sell them.

Avete preso la strada sbagliata. Per arrivare all'autostrada, dovete tornare indietro e prendere la terza uscita alla rotonda. Poi, al semaforo, girate a destra e andate dritti.

You took the wrong way. To get to the highway, you have to come back and, at the roundabout, take the third exit. Then, at the traffic light, turn right and go straight.

164. vero/giusto/corretto – real/true/truth/right/exact/fair/just

Tutto quello che hai sognato non è vero, calmati! Era soltanto un incubo.

Everything you dreamt about is not real. Calm down! It was only a nightmare.

Non ho mai creduto fosse vero che Emilio l'avesse tradita. Il vero problema è che Sonia è paranoica e vede sempre il lato peggiore delle cose.

I have never believed it was true that Emilio had betrayed her. The real problem is that Sonia is paranoid and always sees the worst side of things.

Non dire il vero ti costerà molto, e lo sai, quindi pensa due volte a quello che hai intenzione di raccontare.

Not saying the truth will cost you a lot, and you know it, so think twice about what you are going to say.

Quello che hanno detto non è corretto: le cose non sono andate proprio così.

What they said is not right: things did not go exactly like this.

Questa non è la taglia giusta. Potrei provarne una più grande?

This is not the correct size. Could I try on a bigger size?

Il professore Paoli è severo ma giusto. Giudica sempre i nostri lavori con assoluta precisione.

Professor Paoli is strict but fair. He always judges our work with great precision.

Ciao! Sono arrivata giusto ora, e non vedo l'ora di ballare. Vieni con me?

Hi! I have just arrived, and I can't wait to dance. Are you coming with me?

165. mangiavo/ho mangiato – I used to eat/ I was eating/ I ate/ I have eaten

Quando ero giovane, mangiavo tutto quello che volevo, e non ingrassavo mai. Ora, invece, devo stare molto attento a quello che mangio.

When I was young, I used to eat all I wanted, and I never put on weight. Instead, now I have to pay attention to what I eat.

I miei vicini stavano mangiando in giardino quando il ladro è entrato in casa. Non hanno sentito nulla, e lui ha potuto derubarli senza disturbo.

My neighbors were eating in the garden when the burglar came in. They did not hear a thing, and he robbed them without any trouble.

Ieri sera, abbiamo provato il nuovo ristorante nella piazza davanti a casa. Abbiamo mangiato molto e speso poco.

Yesterday, we tried the new restaurant in the square in front of our house. We ate a lot and spent a little.

Nessuno ha ancora mangiato la mia torta, e non capisco il perché. A me è sembrata molto buona quando l'ho assaggiata.

Nobody has eaten my cake yet, and I do not know why. It tasted good to me when I tried it.

166. era/è stato – It used to be/ it was/ it has been/age

Questa zona della città non era così quando ci sono stato la prima volta, quasi tredici anni fa.

This area of the city was not like this when I came here for the first time, almost thirteen years ago.

Da piccolo, Marco non era mai solo. Sua madre aveva sempre paura che si facesse male o si perdesse.

When Marco was a child, he never used to be alone. His mother was always afraid he could hurt himself or get lost.

Era la prima volta che visitavo il museo, ed è stato più interessante di quanto pensassi.

It was the first time I visited the museum, and it was more interesting than I thought.

Questo gatto è già stato qui, ma non so di chi sia. Se torna, cercherò i suoi padroni.

This cat has already been here, but I do not know who it belongs to. If it comes back, I will look for its owners.

L'era glaciale ha portato i dinosauri' all'estinzione.

The ice era led to the dinosaurs' extinction.

167. smettere – to stop/ to quit/ to give up

Smettetela di fare rumore! Il nonno sta dormendo. Se continuate a urlare, lo sveglierete.

Stop making noises! Grandfather is sleeping. If you carry on screaming, you will wake him up.

Fumi troppo; dovresti smettere. Non ti fa bene alla salute.

You smoke too much; you should quit. It is not good for your health.

Mio cugino, dopo le scuole superiori, ha deciso di andare a Pisa per studiare ingegneria, ma dopo qualche mese, ha smesso perché non gli piaceva. Così, ha iniziato a studiare medicina.

My cousin, after high school, decided to go to Pisa to study engineering, but after a few months, he gave up because he did not like it. So, he started to study medicine.

168. spiegare – to explain/ to unfold/ to deploy/to spread

Non ho capito bene che cosa facciamo domani, ma credo che ce lo spiegheranno non appena arriveremo al luogo di incontro con le guide turistiche.

I didn't understand well what we are doing tomorrow, but I believe they will explain it to us as soon as we get to the meeting point with our tour guides.

Tutte le volte che torno a casa, trovo la coperta sul divano spiegata. Forse il gatto la usa per dormire.

Every time I come back home, I find the blanket unfolded on the couch. Maybe the cat sleeps in it.

I romani spiegavano eserciti numerosi e ben organizzati. È per questa ragione che hanno conquistato così tante terre.

The Romans deployed large and well-organized armies. For this reason, they conquered so many lands.

Il gabbiano è un uccello molto diffuso nelle coste del Mediterraneo. È così elegante che quando spiega le ali assomiglia a un albatro.

The seagull is a very common bird of the Mediterranean coasts. It is a very elegant bird, and when it spreads its wings, it looks like an albatross.

169. arrestare – to stop/ to arrest

Dobbiamo continuare coi lavori di ristrutturazione! Non possiamo arrestarci ora. Deve essere tutto pronto per la parata, quindi dobbiamo fare del nostro meglio.

We need to carry on with the renovation work! We cannot stop now. Everything has to be ready for the parade, so we must do our best.

La polizia pensava di aver arrestato il colpevole, ma, in realtà, avevano preso la persona sbagliata. Da quel momento, hanno iniziato a cercarlo.

The police thought they arrested the culprit, but they actually caught the wrong person. They have been looking for him since.

170. sentire/ascoltare - to hear/to feel/to listen

Questi posti sono i più sfortunati del teatro: non si sente molto bene quello che dicono gli attori.

These are the unluckiest seats of the theater; we can't hear what the actors say too well.

Paola è andata a casa perché non si sentiva molto bene. Spero che non abbia preso l'influenza.

Paola went home because she did not feel well. I hope she did not catch the flu.

Ascoltatemi, per favore: ho bisogno di spiegarvi alcune cose, e dovete prestare la massima attenzione a ciò che dirò.

Listen to me, please: I need to explain some things, and you have to pay close attention to what I am going to say.

171. raffreddore/raffreddare – cold/ to cool

Incredibile, ho il raffreddore da circa due mesi. Potrebbe essere allergia, ma non ne sono sicuro.

Unbelievable, I have had a cold for two months. It may be allergy, but I am not sure about it.

Se non bevi subito il latte, si raffredderà, e non ti piacerà più.

If you don't drink your milk, it will cool, and you won't like it anymore.

172. paese – village/country/nation

Sono nato vicino a Pavia, in un paese di circa mille abitanti. Mi sono trasferito a Milano quando avevo diciotto anni, e ci vivo tuttora.

I was born close to Pavia, in a village of about one thousand inhabitants. I moved to Milan when I was eighteen years old, and I still live there.

I paesi dell'Unione Europea dovrebbero collaborare di più, per garantire a tutti i cittadini condizioni di lavoro e di vita migliori.

European Union countries should collaborate more to guarantee all citizens better work and life conditions.

I bambini dei paesi del terzo mondo soffrono la fame, la sete e non ricevono un'istruzione. Dovremmo lavorare di più per evitare che ciò accada.

Third world nations' children are suffering from hunger and thirst, and they do not receive any education. We should work more in order to stop this from happening.

173. minuto – minute/moment/tiny/puny

Possiamo arrivare da voi in un'ora; più precisamente, in un'ora e diciassette minuti.

We can reach you in one hour; more precisely, in one hour and seventeen minutes.

Aspetta un minuto! Non volevo offenderti, torna qui!

Wait a minute! I did not mean to offend you. Come back here!

Nessuno aveva visto quella donna prendere il portafoglio di mia madre perché era molto minuta e si nascondeva bene tra la folla.

Nobody saw that woman stealing my mother's wallet because she was very tiny and managed to hide in the crowd.

Spesso, i bambini di corporatura minuta, quando crescono, diventano forti e robusti.

Often, puny kids become strong and robust when they grow up.

174. gola – throat/gluttony/canyon/gulch

In autunno, molti soffrono di mal di gola, ma non c'è da preoccuparsi.

During autumn, many people suffer from a sore throat, but there is nothing to worry about.

Anche Dante puniva i peccati di gola, ma io non posso fare a meno di mangiare un dolce almeno una volta al giorno.

Dante also punished the sins of gluttony, but I cannot avoid eating something sweet at least once a day.

Le gole montane fanno parte degli spettacoli più incredibili della natura.

Mountain ravines are amongst the most wonderful natural sights.

Il nascondiglio dei criminali era collegato all'esterno da una gola sotterranea.

The criminals' hideout was linked to the outside by an underground gulch.

175. ecco/eco – here/ I see/there/okay

Ecco qui il tuo amico. Lo stavi aspettando da ore.

Here is your friend. You have been waiting for him for hours.

Ora ho capito . . . Ecco chi ti ha detto queste sciocchezze!

Now, I got it . . . I see who told you these silly things!

Non voglio andare via, ecco tutto!

I do not want to go. There you have it!

Capisco, ecco, ma dovresti fare più attenzione a quello che dici e a chi lo dici.

I see. All right. But you should pay more attention to what you say and to whom you tell it.

176. cercare – to look for/ to seek/to try

È tutto il giorno che cerco i miei occhiali. L'ultima volta che li ho visti erano sul tavolo in cucina. Li hai presi tu?

I have been looking for my eyeglasses all day long. Last time I saw them, they were on my kitchen table. Did you take them?

Sono due mesi che cerco lavoro, ma non ho ancora trovato nulla. Se non trovo un lavoro a breve, mi dovrò trasferire a casa dei miei genitori perché non potrò più pagare l'affitto.

I have been looking for a job for two months, but I have not found anything yet. If I do not find a job soon, I will have to move to my parent's house, as I will not be able to pay the rent anymore.

Ho cercato di convincerlo diverse volte, ma non vuole ascoltarmi. Non credo che cambierà idea.

I have tried to convince him many times, but he does not want to listen to me. I do not believe he will change his mind.

177. cellulare – cell phone/ cellular

I nuovi cellulari sono quasi dei veri e propri computer portatili in miniatura: possono mandare e ricevere email, e sono dotati di applicazioni che ti permettono di scrivere documenti e leggere i file in pdf.

New cell phones are almost mini laptops: they can send and receive emails, and they come with apps that allow you to write documents and read pdf files.

La divisione cellulare inizia subito dopo la fecondazione, quindi, possiamo subito parlare di una nuova vita.

Cellular division starts immediately after the fertilization, so we can immediately talk about a new life.

178. fatto – fact/event/done/made/built

Dobbiamo basarci sui fatti, e non sulle supposizioni per capire che cosa sia realmente successo.

We have to deal with facts and not suppositions to understand what really happened.

Questa mattina mi è capitato un fatto molto strano: ho incontrato una persona che mi assomigliava molto e che mi ha chiesto il mio nome.

This morning, a weird fact happened to me: I met a person who looked like me and asked me my name.

Quando avrete fatto il vostro dovere, potrete parlare.

When you will have done your duties, you will be able to speak.

La cosa più importante per fare un buon tiramisù è scegliere i biscotti giusti e utilizzare la dose corretta di caffè.

The most important thing to make a good tiramisu is choosing the right cookies and using the correct coffee dose.

Tutti questi palazzi sono stati fatti nei primi anni dell'Ottocento.

All these buildings were made at the beginning of the nineteenth century.

179. grasso – plump/fatty/fat/oily

Dopo le vacanze di Natale, ho deciso di mettermi a dieta perché mi sento troppo grasso.

After the Christmas holidays, I decided to go on a diet because I feel too fat.

I ragazzi oggi consumano molte pietanze ricche di grassi, soprattutto perché mangiano spesso cibo spazzatura. Questo comportamento porta all'obesità.

Nowadays, young people eat a lot of fatty foods, especially because they often eat junk food. This behavior leads to obesity.

Se mangi della carne grassa, non dimenticarti di includere della verdura. Così, otterrai un piatto bilanciato.

If you eat fatty meat, don't forget to include vegetables. This way, you will get a balanced dish.

Ho provato un nuovo sciampo per capelli grassi, ma non mi sembra che funzioni molto bene.

I tried a new shampoo for oily hair, but it does not seem to work very well.

180. intelligente – bright/clever

Si crede che l'uomo sia l'essere più intelligente della Terra. Tuttavia, considerati i danni che sta causando, non ne sarei così certo.

Man is judged as the most intelligent living being on Earth. However, considering the damages he has been causing, I would not be so sure.

Di tutti i miei studenti, Sara è sicuramente la più intelligente.

Among all my students, Sara is surely the smartest.

Per il tuo compleanno sto cercando un regalo intelligente non la solita crema per il corpo.

I am looking for a clever gift for your birthday instead of the usual body cream.

181. macchina – car/machine

Non ricordo dove ho parcheggiato la macchina, e sono in ritardo. Forse dovrei prendere un taxi.

I do not remember where I parked the car, and I am late. Maybe I should get a cab.

Abbiamo visitato le vecchie fabbriche della regione e vistp molte macchine che non vengono più utilizzate. Ci hanno spiegato a che cosa servivano.

We visited the old regional factories and saw many machines that are not used anymore. They told us what they were used for.

182. negozio – shop/store

Il centro commerciale che stanno costruendo dallo scorso mese, e che sarà completato entro la fine dell'anno, avrà centinaia di negozio di tutti i tipi, e sarà il più grande della nazione.

The mall they have been building since last month, which will be completed by the end of the year, will have hundreds of different shops and be the biggest of the country.

183. oggi – today/nowadays

Non so che cosa farò oggi. Il tempo non è buono. Forse resterò a casa a leggere o a guardare un film.

I do not know what I will do today. The weather is not nice. Maybe I will stay at home, reading or watching a movie.

Oggi, sono tanti i problemi che dobbiamo affrontare nel mondo: criminalità, violenza, e ignoranza.

Nowadays, many are the problems we have to face in this world: criminality, violence, and ignorance.

184. parlare – to speak/to talk/to make a speech/to confess

Potrai parlare quando avrai letto tutto sulla questione. Per il momento, non ne sai più di tanto, perciò non esprimerti.

You will be allowed to speak when you will have read everything about the matter. For now, you do not know much about it, so don't say anything.

È importante parlare ai bambini sin dai primi mesi di gravidanza. Ciò aiuta a creare un legame forte con la madre.

It is important to talk to children since the first months of pregnancy. This helps to create a strong relationship with the mother.

Il presidente parlerà questa sera alla nazione.

Tonight, the president will be speaking to the nation.

Dopo essere stato arrestato, l'uomo ha parlato: è stato lui a commettere entrambi gli omicidi.

After he was arrested, the man confessed: he had committed both murders.

185. ripetere – to repeat/to say something again/to keep happening

Dopo aver letto le istruzioni, ho ripetuto il processo più volte, ma il macchinario non ha comunque funzionato. Forse è difettoso.

After I had read the handbook, I repeated the process many times, but the machine did not work. Maybe it is faulty.

Scusi, non ho capito. Potrebbe ripetere più lentamente l'ultima frase che mi ha detto?

Sorry, I did not understand. Could you please repeat more slowly the last sentence you told me?

Certi disastri naturali continuano a ripetersi, e questo è causato dal surriscaldamento globale.

Certain natural disasters keep happening, and this is probably caused by global warming.

186. ufficio – office/department

Dopo che verrò promosso, avrò anche un nuovo ufficio all'ultimo piano dell'edificio, che sarà molto più grande. Avrò anche la mia segretaria personale.

After I will be promoted, I will also have a new office on the last floor of the building, and it will be much bigger. I will have also a personal secretary.

La sua richiesta è stata inoltrata all'ufficio di competenza. Se non riceverà una chiamata o non le sarà inviata una comunicazione entro una settimana, la preghiamo di ricontattarci.

Your request has been forwarded to the proper department. If you will not receive a call or you will not be sent a communication within a week, please contact us again.

187. viaggio – travel/trip/journey/I travel

Il viaggio da Milano a Vienna è stato più lungo del previsto perché la macchina si è guastata e abbiamo dovuto aspettare che la aggiustassero.

The trip from Milan to Vienna was longer than we thought because the car broke down and we had to wait until it was fixed.

La scuola ha organizzato una bellissima gita alle cascate. Eravamo in tanti, ma è andato tutto molto bene.

The school organized a wonderful school trip to the waterfalls. We were many people, but everything went fine.

Qualche anno fa, ho fatto un viaggio in Perù. Avevo prenotato un albergo solo per la prima notte. Giorno per giorno, decidevo cosa fare.

Some years ago, I took a trip to Peru. I only booked a hotel for the first night, and then decided what to do day by day.

La vita è un viaggio che ti porta lontano. Sono tante le esperienze che farai. Ci saranno momenti belli e momenti brutti, ma devi vivere sempre con grande entusiasmo perché la vita è una sola.

Life is a journey that takes you far away. You will have many experiences. There will be good and bad moments, but you will always have to live with great enthusiasm because you only get one life.

Viaggio molto per lavoro, e quando sono in ferie amo stare a casa e passare del tempo con la mia famiglia.

I travel a lot for work, and when I am on holiday, I love to stay at home and spend time with my family.

188. il braccio/le braccia/i bracci – the arm/ the arms

Se alzi il braccio, posso curarti la ferita.

If you raise your arm, I can heal your wound.

Ieri ho fatto il trasloco nella nuova casa. C'erano così tante scatole. Ora mi fanno male le braccia.

Yesterday, I moved into my new house. There were so many boxes. Now, my arms hurt.

Mani in alto! Lei è in arresto.

Arms up! You are under arrest.

I bracci meccanici si sono rotti e si è fermata tutta la catena di montaggio.

The robotic arms broke down, and all the assembly line stopped.

189. la mano/le mani – the hand/the hands

Prendi la mia mano e tirati su.

Take my hand and stand up.

Batti le mani e salta!

Clap your hands and jump!

190. il dito/le dita – the finger/the fingers

L'anulare si chiama così perché è il dito su cui porterai l'anello, dopo esserti sposato.

The ring finger is called that because it is the finger where you will wear your ring after you will be married.

Le dita della mano sono cinque, come quelle del piede.

The hand fingers are five, just like the foot ones.

191. il fine/la fine – the scope/the end

Il fine di questo corso è dare le conoscenze di base della cucina italiana e dei suoi piatti principali.

The scope of this course is to give you some basic knowledge of the Italian cooking and its many dishes.

Alla fine di questa giornata, sarò molto stanco, e vorrò solo andare a dormire.

At the end of this day, I will be very tired, and I will only want to go to sleep.

192. il capitale/la capitale – the assets/the capital

Il capitale della compagnia è stato investito lo scorso anno e sarà bloccato per i prossimi due anni.

The company's assets were invested last year and will be blocked for the next two years.

La capitale dell'Italia, Roma, è una delle città più belle al mondo.

The capital of Italy, Rome, is one of the most beautiful cities in the world.

193. il cero/la cera/c'ero/c'era – church candle/wax/I was there/she was there/there was

Nella vecchia chiesa, c'era un cero molto vecchio che nessuno aveva mai acceso. Un giorno decisero di accenderlo ma si dimenticarono di spegnerlo. Così, il giorno dopo, c'era solo la cera sciolta.

In the old church, there was an old candle that nobody ever lighted. One day, they decided to light it but forgot to blow it out. So, the day after, there was only the melted wax.

Ieri sera, sono andato alla festa di Marco, ma Beatrice no. Ci sono rimasto male.

Yesterday, I went to Marco's party, but Beatrice did not. I was not happy about it.

194. perdòno/pèrdono (consider that you will not find the accent generally; it is only to make you understand the different pronunciation) – I forgive/forgiveness/they lose

Quello che mi hai fatto è stato brutto, e ho sofferto molto, ma ti perdono.

What you did to me was very bad, and I suffered a lot, but I forgive you.

Il perdono è un elemento fondamentale per la pace interiore. Non vivrai mai felicemente se non impari a perdonare.

Forgiveness is essential for the interior peace. You will never live happily if you don't learn how to forgive.

Non dargli i biglietti del concerto; perdono sempre tutto.

Do not give them the concert tickets; they always lose everything.

195. il pianto/io pianto/la pianta – the crying/the pain/I plant/the plant/the diagram

Eravamo nel bosco a fare una passeggiata quando abbiamo sentito il pianto di un bambino in lontananza. Siamo andati a cercarlo e, fortunatamente, lo abbiamo trovato. Si era perso.

We were taking a stroll in the woods when we heard the crying of a child in the distance. We went looking for him and, luckily, we found him. He got lost.

Ha pianto per la morte della sorella. Non ha mai ritrovato la forza per andare avanti.

She cried for her sister's death. She has never found the strength to move on.

Ogni primavera, pianto un nuovo albero da frutto in giardino. La pianta che è cresciuta di più in questi anni è il ciliegio.

Every spring, I plant a new fruit tree in the garden. The cherry tree is the plant that has grown up the most during these years.

Non possiamo perderci se seguiamo la pianta dell'edificio.

We can't get lost if we follow the building map.

196. piano/la piana – flat/slow/quietly/the floor/the plan/plain

Per lavorare la pasta, è necessario utilizzare un tavolo piano e grande.

To knead the dough, it is necessary to use a flat and big table.

Spostiamolo piano, o potremmo romperlo.

Let's move it slowly, or we might break it.

Tutti entrarono piano, senza fare rumore. Nessuno voleva svegliare i genitori di Marco che dormivano al piano di sopra.

Everybody got inside quietly, without making any noise. Nobody wanted to wake up Marco's parents, who were sleeping upstairs.

Il piano per la fuga non era stato perfezionato, e così tutta la banda fu arrestata dalla polizia poche ore dopo il furto.

The escape plan was not perfect, so all the gang was arrested by the police a few hours after the theft.

La piana è esposta al sole tutto il giorno, e quindi è necessario piantare delle piante che resistano alla luce e alle temperature calde che caratterizzano questa zona.

The plain is exposed to sunlight all day long, so it is necessary to plant plants that can stand the light and the high temperatures that characterize this area.

197. il metro/la metro – the meter/the subway

Prima di andare al negozio di mobili, dobbiamo prendere le misure. Il problema è che non trovo il metro. Lo hai visto?

Before going to the furniture store, we have to take the measures. The problem is that I can't find the meter. Have you seen it?

La metro di Londra è la più antica d'Europa. Ci sono molte linee, alcune delle quali sono molto profonde. La Northern Line ha la stazione più profonda della città.

The London subway is the most ancient one in Europe. There are many lines, some of which are very deep. The Northern Line has the deepest station in the city.

198. il rosa/la rosa – the pink color/the rose

Il rosa è il colore che piace di più alle bambine, è il colore dei maialini, ed è quello che preferisco.

Pink is the color little girls love the most, it is the color of piglets, and it is the color I prefer.

Un mazzo di rose rosse è il classico regalo che le donne ricevono per il giorno di San Valentino. A me piacciono di più quelle bianche, ma nessuno me ne ha mai regalate.

A red roses bouquet is the common gift women receive on Valentine's Day. I love the white ones, but nobody ever got me some.

199. il modo/la moda – the way/the fashion

L'unico modo che abbiamo per uscire da questa situazione è cercare di trovare qualcosa che metta tutti d'accordo, ma non sarà facile.

The only way we have to get out of this situation is trying to find something on which everybody agrees, but it is not easy.

La settimana della moda di Milano e quella di Parigi sono due tra gli eventi più importanti del settore della moda. I grandi stilisti non possono mancare.

Milan and Paris fashion week are two of the most important events of the fashion industry. Great stylists can never miss them.

200. il panno/la panna/i panni – the cloth/the cream/the laundry

Per pulire questa superficie, è meglio utilizzare un panno apposito. Si può acquistare in tutti i negozi specializzati.

To clean this surface, it is better to use a specific cloth. You can purchase it in every specialized store.

Mangiare una coppa di gelato con la panna è uno dei più grandi piaceri della vita, soprattutto nelle calde sere d'estate.

Eating a cup of ice cream with cream is one of the greatest pleasures of life, especially during hot summer nights.

Devo piegare i panni e poi andare al lavoro. Ti richiamo più tardi perché sono in ritardo.

I have to fold the laundry and then go to work. I will call you later because I am late.

201. il fronte/la fronte – the front/the forehead

Molti furono i soldati che morirono al Fronte, e noi dobbiamo ricordarli sempre perché si sono sacrificati per la nostra patria.

Many soldiers died at the Front. We must remember them, for they sacrificed their lives for our homeland.

Stasera c'è la festa di fine anno e mi è spuntato un brufolo, proprio al centro della fronte. Sono disperata, e non so come fare. Stai tranquilla; ora proviamo con un po' di trucco. Funzionerà.

It is prom night tonight, and a pimple appeared exactly in the middle of my forehead. I am desperate, and I do not know what to do. Don't worry; we will try with some makeup. It will work.

202. il posto/la posta – the space/the place/the mail/the post office

Nella macchina non c'è abbastanza posto per tutte le valigie, quindi dovremo spedirne alcune. Sono sicura che ci costerà molti soldi, ma non abbiamo altre soluzioni. Domani vado all'ufficio postale e spedisco i vestiti, poi vedremo.

There is not enough space for all the suitcases, so we will have to mail some of them. I am sure it will cost us a lot of money, but we do not have any other solution. Tomorrow, I am going to the post office to mail the clothes. Then, we will see.

Hai controllato la posta? Dovrebbe essere arrivato l'invito al matrimonio di Carlo e Marta. Si sposano a fine luglio, in Calabria, il posto dove si sono conosciuti. Sarà un matrimonio magnifico e molto romantico.

Have you checked your mail? The invitation to Carlo and Marta's wedding should have arrived. They are getting married at the end of July, in Calabria, the place where they first met. It will be a wonderful and very romantic wedding.

203. potere – ability/power

Tutti i maghi e le maghe delle fiabe hanno il potere di far apparire e sparire gli oggetti e le persone.

All wizards and sorceresses of fairy tales have the ability to make objects and people appear and disappear.

Troppi sono i poliziotti che abusano del loro potere. Far rispettare la legge non dovrebbe significare avere l'autorità per infrangerla.

There are too many policemen that abuse their power. Enforcing the law should not mean having the authority to break it.

204. almeno – at least/ if only

Per concludere il tratto nei tempi stabiliti, dobbiamo percorrere almeno 200 chilometri al giorno. Solo così arriveremo in tempo per il festival.

To end the itinerary on time, we have to travel at least 200 kilometers per day. Only this way we will arrive on time for the festival.

La festa era molto noiosa: nessuno ballava, e tutti se ne stavano seduti in silenzio. Ma almeno il cibo era buono.

The party was very boring: nobody danced, and everyone sat in silence. But at least the food was good.

Se almeno non piovesse. Domani potremmo andare al mare e rilassarci un po' dopo questa stressante settimana di lavoro.

If only it would not rain. We could go to the beach tomorrow and relax a bit after this stressful working week.

205. andata – one way/first leg/she has gone

Mi scusi, quanto costa il biglietto d'andata per Milano? Solo andata costa venticinque euro, ma se compra anche il ritorno risparmia dei soldi.

Excuse me, how much is the ticket to Milan? One way costs twenty-five euros, but if you buy the back-and-forth ticket, you can save some money.

Avendo vinto il primo girone, la squadra aveva un piccolo vantaggio. Ma ha finito per sprecarlo perché alla fine, ha perso.

Having won the first round, the team had a small advantage. But they ended up wasting it because eventually, they lost.

Non vedo Giulia, sai dove è andata? Ho bisogno di parlare con lei di una questione molto urgente.

I can't see Giulia; do you know where she went? I need to talk with her about a very urgent matter.

206. cattivo – evil/naughty/negative/terrible

Alla fine, l'antagonista viene sconfitto dall'eroe, e tutto torna come prima.

The evil protagonist of the story is eventually defeated by the hero, and everything is back to normal.

Quando i bambini sono maleducati, spesso ci sono delle ragioni, e punirli può non essere la mossa corretta. È meglio capire i motivi dietro al loro comportamento.

When children are naughty, there are often some reasons, and punishing them could not be the right thing to do. It's better to understand the reasons behind their behavior.

Questo è un cattivo presagio. Meglio lasciar perdere e tornare a casa.

This is a bad omen. We should forget about it and go back home.

Abbiamo passato una bellissima giornata. C'era solo quel terribile odore di pesce fritto che arrivava dal ristorante vicino. La prossima volta, sediamoci dall'altra parte del lago.

We spent a very beautiful day. The only thing was that terrible fried fish smell coming from the restaurant nearby. Next time, let's sit on the other side of the lake.

207. dammelo/me lo dia per favore – give it to me!/give it to me please

Quel panino è mio, dammelo!

That is my sandwich, give it to me!

Signora, la sua borsa mi sembra molto pesante. Me la dia, per favore. La porterò io a casa sua.

Madame, your bag seems to be very heavy. Give it to me, please. I will take it to your house.

208. faccelo/ce lo faccia per cortesia – let us doing something/make/do it to us please

Ma che bei cuccioli! Facceli accarezzare! Certamente, ma fate molta attenzione perché sono nati da pochi giorni e sono molto delicati.

Look at those beautiful puppies! Let us pet them! Sure, but be very careful because they were born a few days ago and are very delicate.

Per cortesia, le abbiamo chiesto un piccolo favore. Ce lo faccia.

Please, we asked you a little favor. Just do it.

209. digliela/ glielo dica per favore – tell it to him/her!/tell it to him/her please

Siamo venuti qui con lo scopo di dire la verità, quindi digliela!

We came here wanting to say the truth, so tell it to him!

Sono ore che le chiede che cosa le abbia regalato. Glielo dica, per favore!

She has been asking you what you got her for hours and hours. Just tell her, please!

210. vacci/ci vada per favore – go yourself/go there please

Mi porti dell'acqua? Vacci tu, io non posso. Sto annaffiando i fiori.

Would you bring me some water? Go yourself. I am watering the flowers.

Salve agente, laggiù deve esserci un cane abbandonato, ma io ho paura dei cani. Ci vada lei, per favore.

Hello, officer. There must be a stray dog over there, but I am afraid of dogs. Could you please go there?

211. stacci/ci stia pure – stay there if you like/you can stay here if you like

Se vuoi stare qui, stacci! Io me ne vado a casa perché ho sonno.

If you want to stay here, stay here then! I am going home because I am tired.

Signore, non ho altri appuntamenti dopo di lei, quindi ci stia pure quanto vuole.

Sir, I do not have any other appointments after you, so you can stay here as much as you want.

212. sappi/sappia – know/please be aware

Tu continui a non ascoltarmi, ma sappi che tra dieci minuti me ne vado e tu vieni con me.

You keep not listening to me, but you should know that I am leaving in ten minutes and that you are coming with me.

Signora, sappia che il mio staff e io siamo qui per aiutarla, quindi si senta libera di chiedere qualsiasi cosa di cui ha bisogno.

Madame, please be aware that my staff and I are here to help, so feel free to ask whatever you need.

213. essere – be/be please

Sii la persona migliore che tu possa diventare!

Be the best person you can!

Sia gentile con lui, professore; il ragazzo ha avuto dei problemi recentemente, ma sta cercando di risolverli.

Please, professor, be nice with him; the guy has had some problems recently, but he is trying to sort them out.

214. abbi/abbia – be/have please

Sappiamo che la situazione è molto difficile, ma abbi coraggio. Sono sicuro che con il tempo tutto si aggiusterà.

We know that it is a very hard situation, but be brave. I am sure time will fix everything.

Signora, abbia fiducia. Troveremo la sua borsa. Deve essere qui da qualche parte.

Madame, don't lose faith. We are going to find your bag. It must be here somewhere.

215. settimana/settima – week/seventh

Questa è la settima settimana che lavoriamo con il vostro team, e siamo molto soddisfatti di come stanno andando le cose. Siamo collaborando tutti in modo eccezionale e, oltretutto, stiamo facendo un ottimo lavoro.

This is the seventh week we are working together with your team, and we are very satisfied about how things are going. We are all wonderfully cooperating and doing a great job.

216. successo – success/achievement/approval/happened

Il successo di questo prodotto è dovuto alla sua efficacia e al suo prezzo. Batteremo sicuramente la concorrenza.

The success of this product depends on its effectiveness and price. We will beat our competitors.

È vero che i successi personali dipendano dalla tenacia di una persona, ma anche dalla sua fortuna.

It is true that personal achievements depend on one's perseverance, but they also depend on fortune.

Questo film non ha avuto molto successo per la critica, ma a me è piaciuto molto.

This movie has not received a big approval from the critics, but I liked it a lot.

Se avessi capito che cosa è successo, non ti starei facendo così tante domande. Quindi smettila di dirmi che lo so perché io non so nulla.

If I had understood what happened, I would not be asking you so many questions. So, stop telling me that I know it because I do not know anything.

217. tipo – type/model/dude/character

Quale tipo di attività all'aperto ti piacerebbe fare? Il nostro hotel offre un ventaglio di possibilità, e puoi scegliere quella che vuoi. Dovrai soltanto prenotarti in anticipo.

Which type of outdoor activity would you like to do? Our hotel offers many opportunities, and you can choose what you want. You should only book it in advance.

L'ultimo tipo di computer portatile che ho comprato era migliore di quello precedente.

The last laptop model I bought was better than the previous one.

Sai chi è quel tipo laggiù, quello con la maglia verde? Vorrei tanto conoscerlo.

Do you know that dude over there, the one with the green T-shirt? I would love to meet him.

Ieri ho visto Luigi al bar che faceva l'aperitivo con degli amici. Dopo il secondo spritz, si è messo a cantare, e tutte le persone nel bar hanno iniziato a cantare con lui. Che tipo!

Yesterday, I met Luigi at the bar. He was having an apéritif with some friends of his. After the second spritz, he started to sing, and everybody at the bar started to sing with him. He is quite a character!

218. storia – history/story/matter/relationship/lie

Studiare la storia è molto importante perché è un modo per capire gli errori commessi nel passato, per cercare di non commetterli più.

Studying history is very important because it is a way to understand past mistakes, trying not to repeat them.

Leggere delle storie ai bambini è essenziale per il loro sviluppo del linguaggio, ma anche per quello mentale.

Reading stories to children is essential for their language development, but also for their mental one.

La storia tra Sandra e Pietro è finita nel peggiore dei modi: lei ha incontrato un altro uomo ed è andata a vivere con lui. Pietro non ha ancora superato lo shock.

The relationship between Sandra and Pietro ended in the worse way possible: she met another man and went to live with him. Pietro has not got over the shock yet.

Non raccontarmi le solite storie. Sono ore che ti chiamo ma il tuo cellulare è spento. Dimmi la verità o me ne vado.

Do not tell me your usual lies. I have been calling you for hours, but your cell phone was switched off. Tell me the truth, or I am leaving.

219. colpa – fault/mistake/sin

Mia zia mi ha prestato la sua macchina, ma mentre tornavo a casa uno non ha visto il semaforo rosso e mi è venuto addosso. Fortunatamente, non ci siamo fatti nulla, e, grazie a Dio, non è stata colpa mia. Così, mia zia non si è arrabbiata con me.

My aunt lent me her car, but while I was coming back home, a car did not see the red light and hit me. Luckily, nobody got hurt and, thank God, it was not my fault/mistake. So, my aunt did not get mad at me.

Siamo una società moderna e civilizzata, ed è assurdo che le colpe dei padri ricadano ancora sui figli.

We are a modern and civilized society. It is absurd that fathers' sins still fall upon their sons.

220. casino/casino – mess/trouble/casino

Questa stanza è un casino. Se non la metti a posto, stasera non esci. Quindi, l'unica possibilità che hai per uscire con i tuoi amici è mettere tutto in ordine.

This room is a mess. If you do not tidy up, you are not going out tonight. So, the only chance you have to join your friend tonight is to put everything in order.

Siamo nei casini. Mia madre ha chiamato tua madre, e hanno scoperto che ieri sera non eravamo a dormire da Sofia, ma che eravamo alla festa. Credo che sarò in punizione per molto tempo, e lo stesso vale per te.

We are in trouble. My mother called your mother, and they found out that yesterday night we were not at Sofia's house, but that we were at the party. I think I will be grounded for a long time, and the same goes for you.

Non sono mai stato in un casinò perché non mi piace scommettere denaro, ma è un'esperienza che voglio provare almeno una volta nella vita.

I have never been in a casino, and that is because I do not like betting. However, it is an experience that I want to try at least once in my life.

221. acqua/acquazzone – water/rain

Signore, gradisce un po' d'acqua? Frizzante o naturale?
Sir, would you like some water? Sparkling or still?

Non ho potuto guidare per via di quell'acquazzone. Così, mi sono fermato, e ho aspettato un'ora, e, quando ha smesso, sono ripartito.
It rained so hard I could not drive. In fact, I stopped my car, and I waited for an hour. When it stopped raining, I drove off.

222. ripartire – to leave again/ to take off again/to share

Ero appena tornato da un viaggio in Perù, dove avevo aiutato una piccola comunità a costruire delle scuole per bambini quando mi chiamarono per andare in un villaggio africano dove avevano bisogno di aiuto per costruire dei pozzi. Così, ripartii.
I had just come back from a trip in Peru, where I helped a small community to build some schools for their children when they called me to go to a small African village, where they needed my help to build some wells. So, I left again.

Stavamo viaggiando da quasi due ore in autostrada quando la macchina si è fermata improvvisamente. Ci siamo accostati e abbiamo spento il motore. Abbiamo chiamato un meccanico di un paese vicino e, quando è arrivato, la macchina funzionava di nuovo.

We were traveling for almost two hours on the motorway when the car suddenly stopped. We pulled over and switched the engine off. We called a mechanic from a village nearby, and when he got there, the car started to work again.

Durante il viaggio, i turisti avevano perso degli zaini con il pranzo, e così si sono ripartiti con quello che era rimasto. Arrivati in albergo, avevano molta fame, e così hanno mangiato presto.

During the trip, tourists lost their lunch bags. So, they shared what was left. Once at the hotel, they were so hungry they had dinner very early.

223. centro – center/middle/downtown

Tu credi di essere il centro del mondo, ma non è così. Siamo in molti su questo pianeta, e dobbiamo aiutarci a vicenda senza essere egoisti.

You think you are at the center of the world, but it is not true. We are so many on this planet, and we must help each other without being selfish.

Nel centro della stanza, c'era un tavolo con un bellissimo vaso sopra. Dentro al vaso, c'erano dei fiori freschi e molto profumati.

In the middle of the room, there was a table with a wonderful vase on it. Inside the vase, there were fresh and scented flowers.

Ciao, come va? Volevo dirti che oggi vado a fare un giro in centro. Ti va di venire con me? Potremmo andare a dare un'occhiata al nuovo negozio di scarpe che ha aperto la scorsa settimana.

Hi, how is it going? I wanted to tell you that I am going downtown. Would you like to come with me? We could go have a look at the new shoe shop that opened last week.

224. foglio – sheet of paper/document/layer

Quanti fogli ci serviranno per stampare questi file?

How many sheets of paper do we need to print these files?

Signora, compili il foglio scrivendo nome, cognome, luogo, e data di nascita. Poi firmi in fondo, per cortesia.

Madame, fill in this document by writing your name, last name, place, and date of birth. Then, sign beneath, please.

Questi mobili sono fatti in fogli di compensato.

This furniture is made of layers of plywood.

225. giorno/giornata – daytime/day

In una settimana, ci sono sette giorni, in un mese ce ne possono essere trenta oppure trentuno, e in un anno, ci sono trecentosessantacinque giorni.

In a week, there are seven days, in a month thirty or thirty-one, and in one year, there are three hundred and sixty-five days.

Dopo il viaggio, ho problemi con la differenza di orario: dormo di giorno e sto sveglio di notte.

After the trip, I have had problems with the jet lag: I sleep during the day, and I lie awake at night.

Domani sarà una giornata speciale: è il compleanno della mia migliore amica, e le ho organizzato una festa a sorpresa.

Tomorrow it will be a special day. It's my best friend's birthday, and I organized a surprise party for her.

La gara sarà suddivisa in tre giornate: nella prima giornata gareggeranno le donne, nella seconda gli under 30 e nella terza gli over 30.

The competition is divided in three days: in the first day, women are competing, in the second one, the under 30, and in the third one, the over 30.

226. tagliare/ritagliare – to cut/to slice /to cut again/to cut out/to set aside

Per tagliare la carta, puoi usare delle forbici. Non hai bisogno di usare il taglierino.

You can use scissors to cut the paper. You do not need to use a box cutter.

Puoi tagliare il pane? Gli ospiti stanno per arrivare, e io mi devo ancora vestire.

Can you slice the bread? The guests are about to arrive, and I still have to get dressed.

Quando ho aperto il pacco con il taglierino, ho tagliato quello che c'era dentro. Che sciocca!

When I opened the box with the box cutter, I cut what was inside. Silly you!

Questo pezzo non va bene. Ritagliane un altro e cerca di seguire le istruzioni.

This piece is not okay. Cut another one and try to follow instructions.

I bambini amano colorare, disegnare, e ritagliare le figure dei libri.

Children love coloring, drawing, and cut out the figures of the books.

Lavoro troppo, e non riesco mai a ritagliarmi del tempo libero. Tra qualche mese cambierò lavoro, e spero davvero che le cose vadano diversamente.

I work too much, and I am never able to set aside some free time. In a few months, I am going to change jobs, and I really hope things will change.

227. giacca – jacket/suit

Molti locali, all'ingresso, hanno un guardaroba dove puoi mettere le giacche quando arrivi. Qualche volta è gratis, delle altre devi pagarlo.

Many clubs have a cloakroom at the entrance, where you can put your jacket when you arrive. Sometimes it is free, others you have to pay for it.

Ci sono molti lavori che obbligano gli uomini a indossare giacca e cravatta, ma non credo che sia giusto: ognuno dovrebbe sentirsi libero di vestirsi come vuole.

There are many jobs that force men to wear a suit and a tie, but I do not believe it is right, as everyone should feel free to wear what they prefer.

228. se tornerai-torni/andrò-vado – if you come back/I will go

Se tornerai da me urlando come hai fatto questa mattina, andrò alla polizia. Puoi starne certo.

If you come back screaming as you have done this morning, I will go to the police. You can be sure of that.

Se torni a trovarmi, vado a comprarti uno di quei panini che abbiamo mangiato ieri sul lago.

If you come back to visit me, I will go buy you one of those sandwiches we ate yesterday at the lake.

Se torni a casa, io me ne vado. Quindi, per favore, rimani dove ti trovi ora.

If you come back home, I will leave. So, stay where you are now, please.

229. se avessi più denaro/andrei – if I had/I would go

Se avessi più denaro, andrei a visitare ogni parte del mondo, dalla più bella alla più brutta, dalla più vicina alla più lontana, senza mai tornare a casa. Passerei la mia vita a viaggiare.

If I had more money, I would go to visit each part of the world, from the most beautiful one to the ugliest one, and from the nearest to the farthest. I would never come back home, but spend the rest of my life traveling.

230. se avesse studiato/avrebbe superato – if he had studied/he would have passed

Se avesse studiato di più e con più concentrazione, avrebbe passato il suo ultimo esame all'università, con l'opportunità di laurearsi a marzo. Questo gli avrebbe permesso di fare quel viaggio estivo che desiderava fare. Ora deve aspettare la prossima sessione di esami, e, se tutto andrà bene, potrà laurearsi a settembre. Però per il viaggio dovrà aspettare qualche mese.

If he had studied more and with more concentration, he would have passed his last university exam and had the opportunity to graduate in March. That would have allowed him to go on that summer trip he wanted to do. Now, he has to wait for the next exam session, and, if things work out, he will be able to graduate in September. As for the trip, he will have to wait some months.

231. papà/padre/papa – Dad/father/pop/forefather/founding father

I papà sono spesso più divertenti delle madri: sono quelli che giocano, fanno cose sciocche e che i bambini amano tanto.

Dads are often funnier than moms. They are the ones who play and do silly things, and the ones that kids love so much.

Mio padre lavora in Germania, perciò ci vediamo poco. Torna sempre per le feste e, quando può, anche nei weekend. Quando sarò più grande, potrò andare a trovarlo da solo.

My father works in Germany, and that is why I do not see him that much. He always comes back for the holidays and, when he can, also at weekends. When I am older, I will go visit him by myself.

Padre, a che ora inizia la messa domani? Vorrei confessarmi prima.

Father, what time does the Mass start? I would like to confess before.

Il papa, nel suo discorso domenicale, ha ricordato a tutti noi che dobbiamo essere gentili gli uni con gli altri e che, soprattutto, non dobbiamo dimenticare di compiere atti caritatevoli.

In his Sunday speech, the Pope reminded everyone that we have to be kind to each other, and that, above all, we must not forget to do charitable acts.

Freud e Jung sono i padri della psicanalisi: il loro modo di pensare è ancora moderno, e le loro teorie costituiscono ancora le basi di molti libri.

Freud and Jung are the forefathers of psychoanalysis: their way of thinking is still modern, and their theories are still the basis of many books.

I padre fondatori firmarono la Dichiarazione di Indipendenza il 4 luglio del 1776.

The Founding Fathers signed the Declaration of Independence on July 4, 1776.

232. prendere in prestito/prestare – to borrow/to lend/to serve

Mi scusi, potrei prendere in prestito la sua penna? Devo compilare questo documento e non riesco a trovare la mia.

Excuse me, could I borrow your pen? I have to fill in this document, and I can't find mine.

Non appena finisco questo libro, te lo presto. Devi leggerlo assolutamente: è un capolavoro della letteratura italiana che tutti dovrebbero conoscere.

As soon as I finish this book, I will lend it to you. You must read it: it is an Italian literature masterpiece that everybody should know.

Da circa vent'anni, non è più obbligatorio prestare il servizio militare in Italia. Tuttavia, sono molti i giovani che decidono di arruolarsi per servire il loro paese.

Serving the military service has not been mandatory in Italy for about twenty years. However, many young people decide to enlist to serve their country.

233. sedere/sedersi – to sit/to be seated/someone's behind

Signora, venga, e si sieda al mio tavolo.

Madame, come here to sit at my table, please.

Alla cena ieri sera, tutti sedevano al tavolo del loro ufficio. Secondo me, avrebbero potuto mescolare i dipendenti dell'azienda perché questo li avrebbe aiutati a socializzare con gli impiegati con cui non parlano mai.

At dinner yesterday, everybody was sitting at their office table. In my opinion, people should have been mixed because this would have helped them socialize with other employees of the company whom they never speak to.

Attento! Ti brucerai il sedere se ti siedi lì perché la griglia è ancora calda.

Watch out! You are going to burn your behind if you sit there because the grill is still hot.

234. primo/prima – first/firstly/earlier/in the past/sooner/first of all/before/in front of

Alessandro è sempre stato il primo della classe da quando era alle elementari. Quando è arrivato all'università, si è perso. Forse è successo a causa del fatto che avesse più libertà, o forse per delle cattive amicizie.

Alessandro was always the first of the class since primary school. But when he got to university, he lost himself. Maybe it was because he had more freedom, or maybe because of bad friendships.

Per prima cosa, dobbiamo fare la lista degli invitati. Poi, penseremo a comprare cibo e bevande.

First thing first, we have to make a guest list. Then, we will think about buying food and beverages.

Abbiamo già studiato questo argomento prima, quindi non dovreste avere grandi difficoltà.

We have studied this topic before, so it should not be too difficult.

Prima, quando non c'erano i telefonini, tutti giravano con in tasca delle monetine e una rubrica telefonica, mentre per viaggiare usavano le mappe cartacee. Ora, invece, è tutto a portata di click.

In the past, when cell phones did not exist, everybody had coins and a telephone book in their pockets, while they used maps to travel. Now, everything is just a click away.

Se prendiamo questa strada, dovremmo arrivare prima, ma non ne sono sicuro.

If we take this road, we should arrive sooner, but I am not sure about it.

Cinzia è un'ottima giocatrice di tennis e vince sempre il primo premio.

Cinzia is an excellent tennis player and always wins the first prize.

Prima di tutto, dobbiamo pensare a come uscire da questa situazione. Poi, vedremo di chiarire la nostra posizione.

First of all, we have to think about how to get out of this situation. Then, we will clarify our position.

Da due anni, faccio colazione tutte le mattine a casa. Prima, ero abituato ad andare al bar.

I have been having breakfast at home every morning for two years. Beforehand, I used to go to the bar.

Stavo bevendo un caffè e ho visto Carlo seduto a un tavolino. Improvvisamente, l'ho trovato in piedi di fronte a me. Mi sono spaventata.

I was having a coffee and saw Carlo sitting at a table. Suddenly, he was standing right in front of me. I got scared.

Conclusion

Bene, se stai leggendo vuol dire che sei arrivato alla fine di questo libro. Spero che ti sia piaciuto, e soprattutto che ti sia stato utile.

Instead of giving you the translation of the sentence above, it is your turn to figure it out. If you believe that this is a test or a way to evaluate the job you have done, you are absolutely right. This is not, of course, the only way to test your improvement. The best way should be to find someone to speak with (a native speaker would be great). Then, you will have direct proof of your ability to understand and express yourself.

However, that is not the only thing you can do to check how much you have improved. There are many other opportunities to practice, and it does not matter where you live, if you have Italian friends or acquaintances, or if you can or cannot travel. The Italian movie industry is your perfect chance: you could watch Italian movies in the original language—maybe starting with subtitles to get used to recognizing the words and sentences you learned in this book. Considering that there are many regional varieties of the Italian language—including different inflections, words, and expressions—watching a movie would be another Italian language challenge.

One more important resource is the written language: magazines, newspapers, and books offer many words in varying contexts.

Another thing you can do is try to use the words you learned and make sentences with them. Get inspired by your daily life and play with the words and expressions you read. Luckily, you live in a super-connected world that allows you to find and use lots of online resources.

However, this is not the end; it is just the beginning of your language learning journey. As explained in the introduction, this is not a classic learning manual; instead, it is a source that is available to you whenever you wish to use it. This means that you can start the book again from the beginning or go back to the parts that interested you. Consider this book a sort of "vocabulary in context."

As you would have noticed, this guide offers a huge number of words. The bolded ones are the main elements (the essential ones you need to learn a language), but sentences are full of many others that are as useful as those in the titles. The bilingual method of learning gives you direct access to not only the various meaning of words but also their application in the common context—in a way that a native speaker would use them.

Most of the time, learning manuals have a specific and special purpose: they can be oriented toward grammar or designed for those who want to learn a language for travel, business, or tourism. This is not the case for this book. Here, you have a full immersion into a language, which you can decide to use in any context and for any purpose.

Thus, now that you have a clear overview of the guide's structure, revisit those sentences and words that better suit your learning goals. Read passages again and figure out how you can use them. Repeat them loudly to yourself as it is a good way to test your fluency and pronunciation, which can further be improved by using the Internet.

Lastly, you may have heard about theories that try to find out the minimum number of words a person needs to speak a language. This book does have the answer to that, but it does offer a solution—a source filled with Italian sentences, vocabulary, and, above all, a tool that you can use, shape, and mold for your personal needs.

Good luck with your onward journey into the Italian language.

Buon viaggio!

www.ingramcontent.com/pod-product-compliance
Lightning Source LLC
Chambersburg PA
CBHW070045230426
43661CB00005B/771